MEDIATION AND SOCIETY
Conflict Management in Lebanon

STUDIES ON LAW AND SOCIAL CONTROL

DONALD BLACK *Series Editor*
Center for Criminal Justice
Harvard Law School
Cambridge, Massachusetts 02138

P.H. Gulliver. Disputes and Negotiations:
A Cross-Cultural Perspective

Sandra B. Burman and Barbara E. Harrell-Bond
(Editors). The Imposition of Law

Cathie J. Witty. Mediation and Society:
Conflict Management in Lebanon

MEDIATION AND SOCIETY
Conflict Management in Lebanon

Cathie J. Witty

Medical Anthropology Program
University of California, San Francisco
San Francisco, California

ACADEMIC PRESS
A Subsidiary of Harcourt Brace Jovanovich, Publishers
New York London Toronto Sydney San Francisco

Copyright © 1980, by Academic Press, Inc.
ALL RIGHTS RESERVED.
NO PART OF THIS PUBLICATION MAY BE REPRODUCED OR
TRANSMITTED IN ANY FORM OR BY ANY MEANS, ELECTRONIC
OR MECHANICAL, INCLUDING PHOTOCOPY, RECORDING, OR ANY
INFORMATION STORAGE AND RETRIEVAL SYSTEM, WITHOUT
PERMISSION IN WRITING FROM THE PUBLISHER.

ACADEMIC PRESS, INC.
111 Fifth Avenue, New York, New York 10003

United Kingdom Edition published by
ACADEMIC PRESS, INC. (LONDON) LTD.
24/28 Oval Road, London NW1 7DX

Library of Congress Cataloging in Publication Data

Witty, Cathie J
　Mediation and society.

　(Studies on law and social control)
　Bibliography:　p.
　Includes index.
　1. Justice, Administration of – –Lebanon.
2. Arbitration and award– –Lebanon.　3. Third
parties (Law)– –Lebanon.　4. Justice, Administration
of.　5. Arbitration and award.　6. Ethnological
jurisprudence.　I. Title.　II. Series.
Law　　　347.5692'09　　　79–8863
ISBN 0–12–760850–8

PRINTED IN THE UNITED STATES OF AMERICA

80 81 82 83　　9 8 7 6 5 4 3 2 1

This book is dedicated with love and respect to my mother,
Cecelia M. Witty
who taught me I could be whatever I wanted to be,
and my mentor,
Laura Nader
who believed in me and made it possible.

Contents

Preface ix

Acknowledgments xiii

1
Toward a Theory of Mediation 1
    ADJUDICATION 3
    MEDIATION 4
    PREMISES 20
    PROPOSITIONS 20
    CONCLUSIONS 25

2
Setting 27

3
Family Organization: Tradition and Flexibility 33
    KINSHIP AND COMMUNITY 33
    KINSHIP IN EVERYDAY LIVING 36
    FACTIONS AND KINSHIP 39
    NETWORKS AND CONTINUITY THROUGH KINSHIP 42

4
Conflict Management and Dispute Settlement: The Mediation Process — 45

    SOCIAL INDICATORS: STATUS AND LEGITIMACY — 45
    LEADERSHIP — 48
    A MEDIATED CASE: A PROFILE — 54
    PROCEDURES — 59
    INVESTIGATIONS — 62
    SANCTIONS — 63
    CASE MATERIAL — 66
    WOMEN AND THE DISPUTING PROCESS — 67
    CONCLUSIONS — 73

5
The Police and the Courts — 79

    THE POLICE — 80
    THE COURTS — 89
    ATTITUDES AND CONFLICTING JURISDICTIONS — 90

6
The Waasta-Makers: Intermediation — 95

    POLITICAL BROKERS: THE WAASTA-MAKERS — 95
    ECONOMIC RELATIONS AND REGIONAL INTEGRATION — 100
    WOMEN IN INTERMEDIATION — 101
    CONCLUSIONS — 102

7
Mediation in Urban America — 105

    AN URBAN MEDIATION PROGRAM — 107
    URBAN MEDIATION CASE MATERIALS — 119
    CONCLUSIONS — 123

8
Conclusions — 127

References — 135

Index — 153

Preface

Mediation and Society is a theoretical and empirical inquiry into the nature of mediation and its relation to people, communities, and social systems. Lawyers, social scientists, policy planners, judges, and citizens interested in more responsive legal institutions will find the theory of mediation and the two comparative case studies—one Lebanese and one American—useful in predicting and planning mediational alternatives to district and municipal courts in the United States. The development of a theory of mediation was stimulated by two research experiences focused on mediation as a form of dispute settlement, but located in different cultural settings. Mediation was explored in a rural Middle Eastern village and an eastern metropolitan U.S. community.

Two questions initially directed this theoretical synthesis. First, why is mediation so well developed in the Middle Eastern setting? Second, why does mediation also work effectively in an urban American setting which, superficially at least, seems so culturally different from Middle Eastern society? To answer these questions and the host of corollary questions produced by the cross-cultural data on mediation, it was clear that any analytical model must deal with (*a*) the latent and manifest functions that mediation fulfills within a social group, and (*b*) the relationship between types of dispute settlements and patterns of community production, social class, and social values. With projected answers to these difficult issues, some preliminary answers could then be generated to deal with the central question: What are the social and political variables necessary for successful mediation, whether it is indigenous or carefully implemented through design?

In the Middle East, mediation is a process of resolving and minimizing interpersonal conflict that is intimately connected to the social fabric of people's everyday lives. Mediation is a living, natural, and satisfying process in this setting. In comparison, many Americans no longer have available to them such indigenous, responsive methods of resolving disputes, and they must rely primarily on a bureaucratic court system that is impersonal, unresponsive, expensive, and personally unsatisfying.

Chapter 7 supplements the extensive Middle Eastern dispute materials with a descriptive and analytical look at successful mediation at work within a heterogeneous urban American community. The limited but growing American experience with interpersonal mediation provides some encouraging answers to questions about viable and creative alternatives to the legal apparatus of both large-scale and growing bureaucratic states.

A cross-cultural exploration, focusing on the Middle Eastern mediational system but noting parallels and contrasts with a successful urban American mediation project, specifically offers rich clues for planning and implementing more effective and satisfying methods of dispute settlement appropriate to American culture. Exploring the three central issues around mediation also raises important questions about the development of the law and legal systems in general. Analysis of mediation as an integral and necessary component of a dispute settlement system also specifically and directly questions the role of law and adjudication in American society. Although mediation and adjudication are both social processes, the political and personal implications of each are profoundly different. This comparative analysis is offered as one step in the cumulative process necessary in reassessing the personal needs for dispute resolution within communities, and state and national goals in planning for responsive and just policies in the areas of conflict management and the law.

The name of the Lebanese village central to this study is a pseudonym. The name Shehaam is derived from the Arabic *shehaami*, which means "nobility," because it is the term which for me best captures the attitude and character of the people with whom I lived for the 18-month period of research. I will always be grateful to the people of Shehaam who disrupted their lives to make my residence among them more pleasant, productive, and informative. I also owe generous thanks to the Lebanese government for its hospitality during my periods of residence in Lebanon. It is hoped that this work will be of some benefit to the lives of the farmers and workers who have chosen to remain on the land and struggle for their share of an improved quality of life that is so much a part of their everyday thoughts and hopes for the future.

Since the Lebanese research was completed, there have been deep and profound changes in the social and political lives of the people in Shehaam. This description and analysis, therefore, talks about people and lives that have changed dramatically. The political future in Lebanon remains difficult and uncertain. It can only be hoped, at this point, that the life and economy that will eventually replace that depicted here will be better and richer for those who remain.

July, 1979

Acknowledgments

The two periods of research presented here were both supported by fellowships from the National Institute of Mental Health. The Lebanese research, supported by a predoctoral traineeship, covered an 18-month period from 1972 to 1973; the research and evaluation of the neighborhood mediation program, supported by a training grant in public policy, was undertaken during the academic year 1975–1976. I conducted the urban mediation study while a master's candidate in public administration at the John F. Kennedy School of Government at Harvard University. I wish to thank the faculty and dean of that school for providing and encouraging the flexibility necessary to combine such a project with the requirements of the M.P.A. program.

The urban mediation program, like the Lebanese village under analysis, remains unlocated and unnamed for the privacy and protection of the participants. This research could not have been conducted without the openness and cooperation of the program, however, and I must generously thank the program director and the mediation component directors, past and present, for their valuable assistance. They know who they are.

The extensive Middle Eastern research would have been impossible without the contributions of a number of individuals. To Laura Nader, the director of the research, I owe an immense debt of personal and scholarly gratitude for the inspiration, knowledge, energy, and guidance she gave that made this research possible and productive. I also owe special thanks to Elizabeth Colson, Eugene Hammel, Sue-Ellen Jacobs, Harry F. Todd, Jr., Katherine K. O'Connor, Marc Ross, Jane Goodale, Carole Joffe, Philip Litchtenberg, and Judith Shapiro for their editorial and substantive comments on various drafts and presentations of the manuscript.

To Bryn Mawr College, where I have been able to solidify my commitment to interdisciplinary research and theory-building, and where I had a unique learning experience in administration, politics, and the law, I owe a special debt of professional gratitude.

Toward a Theory of Mediation

1

In looking at disputes and the various ways people resolve them throughout the world, it is clear that mediation is a process widely practiced in both traditional and modern societies. Law and courts as Americans know them are only one example of dispute resolution procedures from within a continuum of procedures that include doing nothing or "lumping it" to self-help, negotiation, and arbitration (Felstiner, 1974, 1975; Galanter, 1974; Hirshman, 1970).

Legal ethnography has experienced a shift from the study of "law" and debates concerning whether law exists in societies without courts, to the more comprehensive and revealing inquiry into the interface between formal statutory law and alternative forms of dispute settlement. In moving from a discussion of what law is and where it exists to a comparison of the various processes people use to manage and resolve disputes, the social character and style of conflict management has emerged as a central focus of comparative inquiry.

Following Malinowski's (1926) early plea that "the cultural context of a primitive system of rules is equally important, if not more so, than the mere recital of a ficticious active *corpus juris* [p. 125]," anthropologists like Colson (1953), Gluckman (1955, 1965), Pospisil (1958, 1969), Turner (1957), Bohannan (1969), and Nader (1965c, 1969) looked for the nature of law in social processes. Colson broke the tradition of structural studies of formal rules and sanctions by dealing with individuals and their various choices and strategies in a particular dispute. Turner followed with his introduction of analysis of the "social drama" in which strategies, relationships, and individual choices made during the dispute settlement process became important analytical indicators. Nader synthesized these findings and the emergent methodological concerns in legal anthropology by focusing on the cross-cultural styles of dispute settlement. Such ethnographic beginnings have since blossomed into elaborations and specializations in both theoretical and methodological directions. Through the various theoretical and medthodological changes that have marked the growth of legal ethnography, scholars have been increasingly aware that law as an abstract philosophical system of thought promulgated by legal scholars is one thing, and norms and social control derived from within social groups as an expression of social organization and integrity is another (see Nader and Yngvesson, 1974; Nader and Todd, 1978).

One clear outcome of cross-cultural comparison is the recognition that most social systems have conciliatory forms of dispute settlement available to the population. In some such societies formal courts, judges, or lawyers may function only within a formally defined system of adjudication, or in some instances, such as the Zapotec of Mexico (Nader 1965a, 1969), a single person may function as adjudicator, arbitrator, or mediator all in one day. The ethnographic evidence is clear, however, that most societies have a range of procedures and methods through which they resolve disputes and manage personal conflict (Schwartz and Miller, 1964; Black, 1976).

A survey of ethnographic data reveals that as one moves from simple to complex on a scale of societal complexity such as Schwartz and Miller (1964) have proposed, the number of alternatives to courts and the quantifiable presence of formal law decreases; that is, as we grow more complex (or more correctly as we grow more "western"), the *range* of alternatives for settling disputes becomes narrower. Black (1976) has captured this relationship succinctly in his proposition that "law varies inversely with other social control [p. 107]."

Contrary to the arguments of Felstiner (1974, 1975) and others that traditional, indigenous forms of dispute settlement will not work in technologically complex, modern societies, the theory of mediation and the supporting cross-cultural evidence that follows argues that (*a*) societies with the greater number of social alternatives for dispute resolution are as complex as societies where alternatives have been eliminated; or conversely that (*b*) narrowing people's access to various means of resolving conflict is not necessarily a mark of social progress.

Furthermore, if one looks at specific ethnographic examples rather than at scaled variable rankings, it is clear that it is not just so-called "simple" societies that offer mediation as one of a series of alternatives to courts. Countries as modern and culturally diverse as the United States (Beck, 1977; Doo, 1973; U.S. LEAA, 1978), Lebanon (Ayoub, 1965; Rothenberger, 1978; Witty, 1975, 1978), China (Cohen, 1967; van der Sprenkel, 1962), Norway and Sweden (Aubert, 1969; Barnes, 1961; Yngvesson, 1970, 1978), Germany (Schmidt, 1952, Todd,

1972, 1978), Austria (Katz, 1975), Turkey (Starr, 1978a, 1978b), Israel (Cohen, 1965), and Japan (Henderson, 1965) all have local and conciliatory forums for dealing with interpersonal disputes.

In order to begin to analyze the social implications of such mediational forms, specifically in contrast to adjudication, a more detailed look at the principles, values, and functions of adjudication and mediation is in order.

Adjudication

DEFINITION

Law is defined throughout this discussion as a formal body of rules and obligations that have been codified, are enforced by a specialized body, and that derive their legitimacy from the dominant political structure. Procedurally, the enforcement of the law is systematically executed throughout American court systems by means of adjudication. *Adjudication*, as used in this text, follows the definition from Nader and Todd (1978) that states that adjudication refers "to the presence of a third party who has the authority to intervene in a dispute whether or not the principals wish it, and to render a decision with means at his or her disposal, and furthermore to enforce compliance with that decision [p. 11]."

Certainly the daily functioning of the legal and judicial systems is characterized by some discretionary decisions that fall outside this strict definition; pretrial intervention, juvenile diversion hearings, reconciliation hearings for divorce settlements, diversion to a social worker for therapeutic family or individual counseling, or arbitration of housing or school disputes are examples of this type of flexibility. But the principles and values upon which adjudication rests are firmly entrenched in the planning and development of the American judicial system.

PRINCIPLES AND VALUES

From its authority base within the dominant political order and its procedural arena in courts of all jurisdicttions, adjudication functions as a means of choosing between right and wrong. Through the use of precedent, conflicting rules, agreements, and obligations are resolved through comparison with similar situations that have occurred in the past. Decisions about what rules should govern people's behaviors in the future are also made through the application of judicial decision, based on legal philosophy, precedent, and judicial discretion.

The outcome of the adjudication process requires that one party be publicly deemed right and the winner, and that the other be found wrong and publicly deemed the loser. This aspect of adjudication has been identified in literature on dispute settlement as the win or lose, "zero-sum" game that adjudication imposes on all participants (Nader, 1969; Nader and Yngvesson, 1974; Nader and Todd, 1978).

FUNCTIONS

Adjudication can be analytically viewed as a model of formal court control of the behavior of the community. With regard to the criminal law, it is what Packer (1968) has discussed as the "crime control model" based on the value that "the repression of criminal conduct is by far the most important function to be performed by the criminal process [p. 158]." In a similar vein, Black (1976) has defined *law* as governmental social control that constitutes "the normative life of a state and its citizens, such as legislation, litigation, and adjudication [p. 2]." From this perspective, the court assesses and controls the behavior of individuals within its jurisdiction, and imposes sanctions on inappropriate, harmful, or deviant behavior. Courts are granted the license to make such decisions and take such actions by the tacit and presumed approval of the community at large. The national political ideology maintains that such a system is egalitarian and objective in its application of rules to individuals; the law is seen as the protector of the community from individuals who would cause personal, civic, or collective harm. This is the legitimate exercise of rational legal authority in the Weberian sense (Weber, 1925).

Mediation

FORMS

Mediation is defined as the facilitation of an agreement between two or more disputing parties by an agreed-upon third party. This third party is known as a *mediator*. Each party agrees to utilize the services of the mediator(s), but the outcome is the agreement made by the disputing parties; no decision or suggestion made by a mediator during mediation is binding or subject to sanction if ignored. The agreement between parties is binding, however, is enforceable through informal social control, and has legitimacy through community consensus.

Mediators are characterized by a number of traits that are consistent cross-culturally. Mediators are respected, indigenous to the community, generous, even-handed, and not young. They are also invariably men, at least in the public aspects of the process. Mediators may act as individuals or may work as groups of individuals from the community. The groups may be kin, non-kin, or a combination of both, depending on the social structure, type of dispute, and length of the procedure. The cross-cultural data reveal a range of variation with regard to such procedural styles.

The role of mediator may be that of an institutionalized neutral individual. Barton (1919) was one of the first ethnographers to descibe such an individual role in his study of a mediation performed by a *monkalun*, or go-between, among the Ifugao of the Luzon area of the Philippines. The Ifugao go-between is always from the elite, respected *kadangyang* class, is chosen by the plaintiff, and serves as a matter of respect and interest in serving his people; he proceeds back and forth between disputing parties facilitating an agreement. From the Ifugao perspective, peace is only accomplished between families. The mediation process itself is described by Barton in Hoebel (1968) as a period of truce. "It is a period that gives both sides to the controversy a chance to cool off. It avoids that rash and ill-considered action that would be likely to follow the breaking off of diplomatic relations between the two parties [p. 100]."

Another classic account of the institutionalized neutral is the leopardskin chief among the Nuer of the Sudan. Evans-Pritchard (1940) noted that the leopardskin chief

> may also act as mediator in disputes concerning ownership of cattle, and he and the elders on both sides may express their opinion of a case. . . . All he can do is to go with the plaintiff and some elders of his community to the home of the defendant and to ask him and his kinsmen to discuss the matter . . . [p. 293].

In many cultures, mediators work as groups composed of various combinations of relatives and friends of the disputants. The Kpelle moot emphasizes the therapeutic value of ventilating anger in the presence of the community and such an assembled group of mediators. Gibbs (1973) contrasts the Kpelle court proceedings which he describes as "basically coercive and arbitrary in tone [p. 293]," with the *moot*, or "house palaver," which is an "informal airing of a dispute which takes place before an assembled group which includes kinsmen of the litigants and neighbors from the quarter where the case is being heard. It is completely an ad hoc group, varying greatly in composition from case to case [p. 293]." Gibbs draws anaologies between psychotherapy, the moot, and the role of mediators. Ventilating personal grievance and structural tensions in the social system has a very therapeutic effect on individuals. Gibbs also cites Beattie (1957) as another African example of a group process which is open, permissive, supportive, and understanding. Gibbs (1973) goes on to say that "permissiveness in the therapeutic setting (and in the moot) results in catharsis, in a high degree of stimulation of feelings in the participants, and in an equally high tendency to verbalize these feelings [p. 374]." Thus, the constant, open airing of conflict and interpersonal disputes allows people to relieve anxiety; it is therapeutic in the framework of general mental health, both for the individuals and the community.

Gulliver presented, first with the Arusha (1963) and then with the Ndendeuli

(1971), another case in which "disputes between neighbors, and differences in opinion and action affecting the interests of neighbors, were almost invariably treated within the local community [1971, p. 132]." In the Ndendeuli case, disputants rally supporters through their local kinship networks, and non-kin allies are sought as well. There is a ritualized meeting accompanied by beer drinking and a feast. Gulliver (1971) refers to this community meeting as a "moot" in the same fashion as Gibbs. Mediators in this setting act as brokers between the two parties and they are "active in suggesting and pressing positive means of reaching an agreed settlement.... He [the mediator] had no sanction at his disposal, and was a prime exponent of the compromise [p. 137]." In noting the general mediational role of integrating disputes into a social context, Gulliver (1971) concludes by noting that

> moots were also occasions for examining the development and readjustment of neighborly relations and expectations within the changing network, for expressing as well as fulfilling obligations, for acquiring entitlement to future claims, for assistance, and for seeking to further influence and prestige [p. 187].

The cross-cultural literature is rich with data that indicate that mediation and similar informal procedures (i.e., negotiation) based on kinship, interaction, shared values, and common community concerns are utilized within local communities, while formal forms of law, largely adjudicatory, are used locally in exceptional cases or cases involving strangers to be community. Gluckman (1955) was among the first to note that "multiplex membership of diverse groups and in diverse relationships is an important source of quarrels and conflict; but it is equally the basis of internal cohesion in any society [p. 20]." In making the distinction between single-interest, or *simplex*, relations and *multiplex* ones, Gluckman noted that the form of dispute settlement and type of outcome could be predicted. People in multiplex relationships with one another rely on conciliatory outcomes to conflict because they wish to maintain on-going relations and obligations within the community; people in simplex relationship with one another choose punitive or zero-sum decisions as outcomes to disputes because they have no interest in maintaining on-going relations with the other party. Nader and Todd (1978, p. 13) have also discussed this phenomenon and synthesized it in a visually succinct model.

Gulliver (1971) takes specific note of this procedural dichotomy in the Ndendeuli case, where "the processes of dispute settlement with a Ndendeuli local community... followed the mode of negotiation, not that of adjudication [p. 179]." Gulliver further noted that "official institutions were controlled by non-Ndendeuli and represented alien authority to the people.... The people saw little reason to accede or appeal to either external authority, and neither sought to compel the use of the official judicial mechanisms except in certain limited instances... [p. 132]." This tendency toward procedural dichotomy based on conciliatory or punitive outcomes and social identity is well documented in numerous other ethnographic cases (see Doo, 1973; Forman, 1972; Katz, 1975; Ruffini, 1974, 1978; Todd, 1972, 1978; Yngvesson, 1970, 1978).

Middle Eastern legal ethnographers have also documented the separation of local mediation processes from the formal legal system (Ayoub, 1965; Nader, 1965a; Antoun, 1972; Rothenberger, 1978; Starr, 1978a, 1978b; Witty, 1975, 1978). This dichotomy is explored in detail in Chapters 4, 5, and 6.

In general, there are two well-developed forms of mediation that operate in this vast cultural area that spreads across North Africa, north into Turkey, and east as far as Iran. First, there is group *mediation* (see Chapter 4; Rothenberger, 1978); the groups of mediators proceed back and forth facilitating agreements in a process similar to that of the Ifugao go-between. Second, there is *waasta*, or *intermediation*, conducted by one individual (usually a patron, elite, or political broker) for the benefit of particular families under his allegiance (Barth, 1959a; Cunnison, 1966; Peters, 1963, 1977; Fernea, 1970; Jones, 1974; Jongmans, 1973; Khuri, 1975; Obermeyer, 1973; Starr, 1978a, 1978b; Vinogradov, 1973, 1974). *Waasta* making in Lebanon is discussed in Chapter 6, but as in all mediation, both Middle Eastern forms are conducted within a relatively closed cultural and political system, bring honor and respect to the mediators, and self-respect and conciliation to the participants. These two forms of mediation coexist, with variations in procedural style, both within Middle Eastern groups characterized by strong segmentary kinship structures (Barth, 1959a, 1961; Cohen, 1965; Nader, 1965a; Peters, 1960, 1963, 1977; Bujra, 1971), and within groups characterized by less segmentary, more network-organized support groups (Gulick, 1967; Antoun, 1972; Doumani, 1974; Jongmans, 1973; Witty, 1975, 1978).

FUNCTIONS

An examination of the cross-cultural literature, as outlined briefly by some illustrative examples, reveals that mediation performs predictable personal and social functions, regardless of the cultural setting. Mediation allows disputants and their supporters to (*a*) talk in a verbal style that is natural and comfortable; and therefore it is (*b*) mutually intelligible to all the participants; it is (*c*) therapeutic, in that it allows free ventilation of anger and frustration; (*d*) it gives a person an increased sense of power and personal worth because one's neighbors find one's problems important; (*e*) it is readily accessible, quick, and inexpensive, and (*f*) it helps equalize or realign status and interpersonal power struggles by promoting an egalitarian ethic; and finally, mediation (*g*) reestablishes and realigns an individual's place and sense of belonging to the relevant social group, whether it be the family or the community.

Whatever the style, whether it be an African moot or a mediation panel in an urban American community (Doo, 1973; U.S. LEAA, 1978), both parties talk and explain the dispute from their own points of view without any limit on their discourse. Open discussion is not only therapeutic, but makes the proceedings intelligble to all parties and decreases confusion and cultural misunderstanding (see Gibbs, 1963, 1973; Swett, 1969; Collins and Pancoast, 1976; O'Connor, 1977; Speck and Attneare, 1973). All forms of mediation operate directly out of the community, and therefore accessibility and expense do not act as constraints on any portion of the population. Local accessibility acts to lower individuals' frustrations with bureaucratic court structures within the community, and increases an individual's sense of personal worth because interpersonal conflict is dealt with in a personal and responsive manner (see Chapter 7; Lerner, 1979; Nader and Singer, 1976; U.S. LEAA, 1978). Accessibility also reaffirms an individual's place within the family or community group. This function is extrapolated from the function of all group rituals to reaffirm and reestablish group solidarity (Mauss, 1906; Durkheim, 1954). Durkheim (1954) argued that ritual composed the interface between external moral constraints, such as the formal legal system, and the internal feelings and emotional constructs of the individual. This perspective further strengthens the argument that the ritual, therapeutic function of community mediation systems acts to support, socially reaffirm, and psychologically integrate the individual into the community.

In any mediated settlement, an egalitarian ethic is reinforced both manifestly and latently. Each individual is treated equally by the mediation process, symbolic spatial markers of authority and status are nonexistent or neutralized, and differences in wealth and status do not appear to affect the outcomes of mediated settlements. This aspect of mediation is further documented for the Lebanese case in Chapter 4.

Following Gluckman's (1955) observation that conciliatory, egalitarian forms of dispute settlement emerge from culturally homogeneous communities characterized by multiplex relations between individuals, researchers have noted that such traditional communities are also characterized by strong obligations of kinship and by the organization of community production around kinship units. Leadership in such communities tends to be deeply enmeshed in kinship organization and status, so that leaders and elites work for the good of all as well as themselves in maintaining the relative status quo through compromise. They perform this leadership function through a form of authority separate from and decentralized from the dominant national political structure.

In contrast, in communities where men and women compete as individuals in a competitive market economy, the web of kinship obligations is more loosely knit, and individual choice operates in conjunction with kin and non-kin alliances. These communities may be culturally homogeneous, but this shift from group identity to individual identity, accompanied by predictable economic and mobility patterns, characterizes the larger phenomenon of urbanization and westernization. People tend to leave the kinship obligations of the village for the relative independence and autonomy of urban centers, seek jobs independent from small-scale production based on kinship units, and gradually other relatives, usually young, join the migration to the cities. This pattern exhibits considerable variation from cultural area to cultural area, but the effects on dispute settlement are consistent. Community based norms gradually lose legitimacy in favor of the formal national legal system which, in many areas of the world, is imported from western European legal traditions. In many developing nations European legal systems initially functioned to streamline the operations of the economic, monetary, and commercial sectors of the economy; then, with variable speed and effectiveness, the nonindigenous systems spread into other areas of interpersonal relations (see Anderson, 1965b, 1971; Auerback, 1969; Henderson, 1965; Kuper and Kuper, 1965; Doumani, 1974; Galanter, 1976; Magnarella and Turkdogan, 1974; Magavern, Thomas, and Stuart, 1975; Quandt, 1970; Starr and Pool, 1974; Wanda, 1975).

Collier (1979) documents the effect of such differences in leadership, production, and kinship organization in two neighboring communities in the highlands of Chiapas. In the traditional, multiplex, kin production-based community of Zinacantan, "they are constrained to act as mediators because disputants must be reconciled if crucial production and kinship obligations are to be fulfilled [p. 306]." In a nearby community with a competitive, open market system, characterized by western dress and bilingual residents, Collier (1979) notes that

> because the men whose wealth might allow them to become natural leaders feel little pressure to interfere in the quarrels of others, the job of handling local disputes is left to an official who, because the job offers few rewards, prefers to make his own decisions rather than spend time seeking solutions to reconcile disputing parties [p. 306].

Collier succinctly details a pattern that is widespread through the world and one that pinpoints the societal functions of community based mediation. Patterns of personal identity and leadership are decentralized in local communities, people have shared community values and are not very geographically mobile; individuals have a sense of themselves as members of a geographic, ethnic or conceptual, self-defined community (see page 34; Wolf, 1966), and thus have some common bases for resolving their conflicts. Collier also highlights the important point that if elites did not mediate and realign individuals and family conflicts, local production and survival could not continue smoothly.

To complement this summary of the functions of mediation, the principles that underlie the success of mediation in any cultural setting need to be analyzed.

PRINCIPLES

Mediation is a social process that is based on the following principles:

1. Some degree of on-going personal interaction exists between disputants.
2. Both parties are willing to settle in a private forum.
3. Both parties are willing to express personal wants and needs.
4. A shared cultural or community identity exists.
5. A willingness or necessity to continue in a relationship with the other disputing party exists.
6. Both parties believe in the relative egalitarian relationships within the context of the dispute.
7. Intangible social resources such as status, honor, prestige, and personal satisfaction are equal to or more important than tangible resources such as money, property, or land.
8. Reaching an agreement is more important than determining absolute right or wrong.
9. People are more likely to adhere to agreements they understand and have an integral part in making than to agreements that are externally imposed.

Interaction

The first principle of mediation requires *the presence of on-going personal interaction*. Traditional, homogeneous, multiplex communities exhibit intense interaction patterns between community residents. Urban centers or villages with non-kin based, individualized market and personal support systems are increasingly characterized as impersonal, large-scale, and anonymous. Individuals who are no longer enmeshed in tight-knit kinship networks and their concomitant reciprocal social and economic obligations, live in large urban communities surrounded by non-kin neighbors and vast, complex bureaucratic structures that deal with personal, family, social, economic, or business problems. This perception of urban life underlies the argument that although mediation may work in communities where people share a common heritage and know one another in an intimate and comprehensive way, mediational processes have no relevance to modern urban living—particularly American urban living—because American cities are not characterized by shared social values, intimacy, and on-going personal interaction patterns (Danzig and Lowy, 1975; Felstiner, 1974, 1975).

Urban American experiments with mediation in various procedural forms, cross-cultural data on migration patterns to urban centers, and the literature on urban families suggests that urban American life is more than one extreme on a simple evolutionary continuum ranging from family based communities to anonymous urban survival (Moore, 1969; Suttles, 1968; Feldstein and Costello, 1974; Howell, 1973; Ladner, 1971; Stack, 1974; U.S. LEAA, 1978). Furthermore, community organizing experiences and American community mediation programs demonstrate that a sense of community identity and conciliatory dispute settlement can be created or regenerated in urban, heterogeneous communities (see Alinsky, 1969, 1971; Weissman, 1969; Byles and Morris, 1977; Cloward and Piven, 1977; Cochrane, 1971; U.S. LEAA, 1978; Yin and Yates, 1975). Cloward and Piven (1977) highlight the use of unresolved conflict and grievance in their discussion of the welfare rights movement:

> Welfare rights organizing throughout the country relied primarily on solving the grievances of existing recipients as an organizing technique. The approach usually worked to build groups, for grievances were legion. Families were often capriciously denied access to benefits, or failed to receive checks, or received less than they were entitled to, or were arbitrarily terminated, or were abused and demeaned by welfare workers. The promise that such grievances could be solved brought recipients together [p. 297].

In any large urban area there are settled traditional neighborhoods; such neighborhoods were created around racial and ethnic origin or common community experience. There are also areas where individuals are effectively isolated from neighbors and on-going meaningful social interaction, particularly in the inner cities (Srole, Langner, Michael, and Rennie, 1962; Bahr and Garett, 1976; Howell, 1973; Rubin, 1976; Spradley, 1970; Stack, 1974; Wiseman, 1970). The flexibility of community mediation makes adjustment to such varied social conditions politically and administratively possible.

A similar neighborhood, clustering phenomenon exists in city organization in diverse cultural areas. Middle Eastern cities, for example, have been characterized for centuries by sections or quarters that were homogeneously composed of tribal, ethnic, or religious groups; each group lived with people of shared cultural values within their quarter, but in juxtaposition to the myriad of other diverse groups resident within the city walls (Coon, 1958; Abu-Lughod, 1965; Gulick, 1963, 1967; Lapidus, 1967; Schorger, 1969). These similarities in city forms and interactional patterns certainly leave the question of neighborhood identity and the cross-cultural application of mediation open for critical reevaluation.

Willingness

The *willingness to settle in a private forum*, the second principle of mediation, springs from a variety of personal and social motives. In traditional communities where social control prevails over formal law, the willingness to settle disputes internally grows out of a sense of separation from national institutions such as the courts. Internal resolution also grows out of a concomitant feeling that personal disputes are personal matters to be pursued in a private way that strengthens an individual's place in the community. Formal law in traditional settings tends to originate out of a different cultural and ideological base as has been discussed, and is therefore not seen as legitimate or relevant to local social concerns. In the traditional Lebanese village discussed in this volume families recognized the Lebanese state because of its institutionalized enforcement power, but villagers felt the state had no real, legitimate jurisdiction in local disputes.

The willingness to settle in urban American settings comes from personal frustration and cultural distance from the law. In effect, America has generated the cultural distance between individuals and the law that Lebanon and other developing countries have had imposed on them through colonialization and mandate governance. The greater the distance of the cultural life of a community from the dominant "center" of national cultural values, the greater the marginality of that community and its members; formal law appears increasingly irrelevant to cultural and minority groups stigmatized in this way. Law no longer works for individuals in a consensual fashion, but works upon individuals in an external, administrative fashion. Alinsky (1969) spoke of this phenomenon in a general way in noting that

> we are living in a situation where much of life has become depersonalized, anonymous, and abstract, accompanied by a loss of personal identity, yet conversely, we also live in a technological age that has... dramatically personalized a variety of issues ranging from Vietnam to civil rights to urban riots [p. 234].

White working-class American families often feel that the court system costs too much, takes too much time, is too easy on minorities, deviants, and people who do not work, and generally does not understand common working people. There is an increasing sense among the white working class that the law no longer works for them but upon them.

Blacks, and particularly urban Blacks, experience the same alienation from formal law, but in a more overt and personally oppressive way. The Black experience with riot and crowd control, law enforcement, and assistance from the police reinforces those community feelings daily (Black, 1971, 1973; Blauner, 1972b; Chestang 1972, 1976a; Marks, 1971; Stack, 1974). The salient argument, which will be elaborated in the discussion of the propositions that predict successful mediation, is that many Americans, regardless of age, sex, class, race, ethnicity, or place of residence, are dissatisfied with law and "justice" for one reason or another, and are willing to try an alternative if they have some experience or belief that the alternative will work.

Personal Needs

The willingness to express one's personal needs—the third principle—has different origins in traditional and urban settings, but the outcomes can be synonymous. Social life in traditional communities is more personally intense; the network of kin and allies in a person's social world is more dense and interconnected than in urban American life. While it may take urban dwellers longer to experiment with solutions to personal problems because of urban isolation, and while it may take them some time to view the community mediation process with trust because it is a relatively new concept in urban American life, the success and growing interest in mediation programs shows that personalized, responsive methods of dispute settlement succeed in the long run. The emerging literature on wife and child abuse, incest, and other domestic violence also indicates that people are increasingly willing to seek private, informal solutions to chronic personal or community problems. Indeed, many of the participants in the American mediation program (discussed in Chapter 7) expressed an urgent need for a private, nonpublic forum of personal redress. The public attitudes, the cost, the uselessness, and the stigma associated with having to take one's problems to a public institution kept many complainants from dealing effectively with family problems and neighborhood disputes.

Studies of the American court system have noted a statistical rise in domestic-related cases, giving rise to the hypothesis that domestic and interfamily disputes comprise a large portion of urban American conflict; combined with the accumulating data on urban mediation (Chapter 7), such statistics indicate that the docketed court cases may only be the tip of the iceberg. Lempert (1978) notes in reviewing the statistical findings of Friedman and Percival (1976) that

> in 1890 family matters accounted for 19 percent of the judicial docket in San Benito County [California], while in 1970 they accounted for 62 percent of the docket. If one can specify types of cases in which a court acts primarily as a dispute settler and other types of cases in which a court is primarily engaged in routine administration, such data might lead one to conclude that over time the business of courts has come to consist of relatively more routine administration and relatively less dispute settlement [p. 93].

Thus, Lempert not only notes the dramatic increase in family cases on the dockets, but argues that they are dealt with administratively and not as a matter of dispute settlement. It seems clear from this data, as well as other court studies, that the court system is not a forum in which people feel free to express personal needs related to disputes (see Cahn and Cahn, 1966; Swett, 1969; Beck, 1977; Brickman, 1973; Felstiner, 1975; Nader and Singer, 1976; Sarat and Grossman, 1975).

Shared Identity

Traditional settings where mediation is an indigenous process are characterized by *a shared cultural or community identity*—the fourth principle. In such settings, a shared belief system gives rules, obligations, procedures, and sanctions their legitimacy; there is no discrepancy between external and internal systems of moral and political order. One's internal cultural life is synonymous with one's external code of ethics; the congruence results in an individual's integrated identity.

There is another perspective from the individual point of view, however, that characterizes nontraditional, heterogeneous, and ethnically diverse settings. Urban settings are economically and ethnically diverse and require an analysis that deals with individual and social variables. One of the most useful concepts to emerge on ethnic and racial perspectives within a pluralistic society since Barth's contributions to the nature and definition of ethnic groups (Barth, 1969), is the dual perspective on dominant and subordinate cultural groups that has emerged from social work theory and practice; this work is best represented in the work of Chestang (1972, 1976a, 1976b) and Norton (1976, 1978).

Chestang and Norton draw from the experience of social work practitioners to analyze American society from the psychocultural perspective of a minority person. They argue that minority individuals live in two different cultural environments. Chestang (1976a, 1976b) has called these the nurturing environment and the sustaining environment. The *nurturing environment* is that primary cultural space where every individual grows up; it is the emotional, affective aspect of social and psychological space. Norton (1978) notes that it is composed of "those closest and most involved in the determination of an individual's sense of identity [p. 4]." It is the internal cultural area where values are learned, where support is based, and where an individual finds shelter from the outside world.

The outside, external world is the *sustaining environment*. It is multiethnic and multiracial in composition, but in America, it is dominated by a national political and moral order drawn from a northern European heritage. In the sustaining environment, the occupational, public, educational, physical, and economic needs of individuals are competed for and obtained; it is in the external world that we must all work in order to feed, clothe, educate, and develop ourselves and our families.

The less the cultural distance between the nurturing and sustaining environments, as in the traditional cultural community, the more congruent and aligned are the experiences of individuals and communities in the movement back and forth across this boundary. The closer a group is culturally and politically associated with the dominant cultural ruling class, the less the incongruity and dissonance in the daily transition from nurturance to sustenance. Such dissonance will vary with geographic location, for locally any groups may be a minority at any time. An Irish Catholic enclave in a New England Protestant majority community may have cultural congruity problems moving from family to dominant public cultural values, but those same Irish Catholics have a closer tie to the dominant national ruling class than urban Blacks or Hispanics. As Norton (1978) stated the problem, "for many minority groups the conflict grows out of the degree of incongruence between the two systems, since the frames of reference of the minority group, though embedded in and affected by the major society, can be quite different [p. 6]."

The emerging literature demonstrates that there is tension and incongruence among white working-class families based on diffused feelings of personal powerlessness, even though they are economically more privileged than Blacks and other minorities (Gans, 1962, 1974; Coser, 1974; Howell, 1973; Klonoski and Mendelsohn, 1970; Levitan, 1971; Rubin, 1976; Skolnick and Skolnick, 1971, 1974). This is consistent with the political perspective that in a bureaucratic, capitalistic welfare state pervaded by racism, even most whites have very little effective power in changing established patterns of cultural and political dominance (Blauner, 1964, 1972; Cloward and Piven, 1974, 1977). For the minority person, particularly urban Blacks, Hispanics, American Indians, and Asians, two separate cultural systems are in operation. Discussion of this cultural division as a dual perspective grows out a need to analyze a self-defined identity, instead of an analytically defined identity, within the larger political and economic order.

It is a matter of degree, then, in assessing the relative distance of various occupational, racial, and ethnic groups in relation to the dominant political order, and the governmental moral order associated with that political order—the law. Urban American cities and cities in many parts of the world it has been noted, develop ethnic, religious, and racial enclaves where people of similar cultural backgrounds congregate and settle. This fact, and the fact that individuals in local neighborhoods and communities perceive the law, in varying degrees, to be integrated or totally unrelated to their internal personal and cultural lives, become an integral segment of the propositions for successful mediation. People have personal and community needs that are not being met by the legal system, and this makes community dispute settlement processes particularly amenable to change.

Continuation of Relationships

This brings us to the fifth principle of mediation, *the willingness or necessity to continue in a relationship with the other disputing party*. This willingness often grows out of the shared community identity previously discussed. An argument raised against mediation in a complex, urban American setting is that this shared sense of community does not exist in urban centers. The literature is rich, however, with examples of community action and advocacy projects that demonstrate that community spirit can be generated or tapped by threat of action from the outside, or that it exists internally as a natural function of social closeness (see Alinsky, 1969, 1971; Cloward and Piven 1974, 1977; Lerner, 1979; Yin and Yates, 1975).

Clearly there is variation in the degree of interaction and solidarity, and in the geographic size of neighborhood units; some solid, self-identified units may be city blocks in area, while other may encompass only a block or a street. There is also variation along ethnic and cultural lines, as analysis from the dual perspective has emphasized. However, the individual's sense of continuity within some personal group and the belief in the value of continuity at the local level, are important components of the mediation process in a modern urban setting. As has already been noted, since mediation is most directly relevant to interpersonal disputes between people with a high degree of social interaction, such as family members and neighbors, the theory of mediation tells us that implementation of community mediation programs should best begin with those types of cases. The degree to which the mediation process spreads from neighborhood to neighborhood depends on the nature and intensity of the cultural and political distances people maintain from the law. One could predict for a homogeneous ethnic neighborhood that mediation as a family, neighborhood, and community process in American cities would be relatively easy to generate, while multi-ethnic or multiclass residential sections would take more time and more decentralized, smaller unit of organizational structure to insure success. The predictive focus of the propositions for successful mediation that follow deal with this component of the implementation problem in greater detail.

Egalitarianism

Sixth is the principle of the need for *a belief in the relative egalitarian relationships between disputing parties* within the context of the dispute. One of the most frequent misconceptions about mediation is that it can only work among people who are equal in income and status. Such a constraint is certainly not true in traditional communities; mediation functions to equalize status differentials, if only in a specific and local context. People may be of different standing or economic class in a community, but by choosing to mediate they become individuals with a common goal—a conciliatory resolution in a private forum. There are clear economic and social status markers in any social group, but the belief in the mediation process ameliorates a large portion of the differences in a time of open grievance and dispute.

Mediation fulfills the same function in modern urban American society; mediators are skilled in facilitating an atmosphere for both parties to reach a satisfying agreement. All participants sit at the same table on the same physical level, unlike the courtroom where status hierarchies are clearly marked by the ordering of physical space. Assuming that the willingness to settle has brought the disputing parties to mediation, the belief in egalitarian status, real or symbolic, is the most utilitarian posture to take since the parties have agreed to engage in a compromise solution. Sutherland (1949) and Macaulay (1963) among others, have noted the absence of adjudication and legal contract in business dealings and disputes, and Fuller (1968) analyzed the uses and limitations of adjudication with certain types of cases. In labor disputes, business dealings, or whenever on-going relations are necessary after resolution of the conflict, mediation or arbitration—a process by which a neutral third party may make a binding decision if the two parties remain unresolved—will be the preferred mode of settlement (Macaulay, 1963; Simkin, 1971; Wanner, 1974, 1975). In instances where economic gain, assets, and production hang in the balance, the parties are not equal in an absolute economic sense, but each side has a resource or resolution that the other party wants and needs for survival.

Disputants in the mediational context are never allowed to bully or browbeat one another. In both urban and traditional settings mediation focuses on free expression of anger and hostility, but mediators promote equality between the parties during mediation while protecting the complainant against further action or abuse from the accused.

A frequent example of power differential in the urban mediation programs is the husband–wife and female–male relationship. Often working-class women, by their own description, have seen violence and despair in their natal families and neighborhoods, and subsequently see the same characteristics recreated in their domestic unions; various feelings of passivity, powerlessness, hopelessness, or low self-esteem have kept these women from taking preventative or protective action, sometimes for years (see Rubin, 1976). The public nature of the courts is frequently cited by women in an American mediation program as a deterrent to resolution of conflict. The conservative, mainstream view of women's roles in society held by the courts and the men who administer them are also cited as deterrents. One woman, who had been beaten regularly for over 10 years, put it this way:

> "I couldn't go to court. It would make him madder than before and he'd beat me up worse if I did that. I had a friend who finally did that one, because of the kids, and the judge told her to be nicer and more understanding, and he wouldn't beat her so much. So what help is that? Who needs it? Now I just pick up a chair... [personal interview]."

Community mediation offered this woman a chance to dispute with her husband in a fair and monitored setting and to find out what she really wanted as an ultimate resolution; mediation allowed her husband to talk to her about their marriage for the first time in 15 years, and to begin to deal with the pressures he often felt powerless to handle. After two long sessions, this man and woman signed a written agreement realigning aspects of their relationship to mimimize conflict and increase understanding, and he agreed to accept a referral to an alcoholism program in the community. Thus, even though the social and economic status of women and men in this working-class community is very different, the willingness to find a better solution to a chronic problem allowed mediation to be productive in this case; the husband was not punished for his physical assault against his wife, but she did not want him punished, she wanted the behavior to cease, although separation was one of the alternatives clearly discussed between the woman and the mediators.

Egalitarianism as a principle raises the question of the meaning of sanctions in a mediated dispute. If both parties are equal, socially or symbolically, what is the purpose of sanctions and how are they enforced? Traditional communities have common moral standards through which they apply social and personal pressure for redress; such redress is usually in the form of restitution rather than punishment, although extreme cases do generate ostracism, physical punishment, public humiliation, public ordeals, and similar kinds of quasi-punitive resolutions. Mediation cross-culturally is quite varied in this regard because sanctions are clearly a matter of community standards and consensus within which individual disputants have a great deal of flexibility. Whatever the disputing parties agree will satisfy them both is the final, binding solution.

In urban American communities, cultural distance has not only separated people from the law in varying degrees, but it has separated them from each other as well. In such a setting, one effective use of sanctions is as a threat. That is, if a formal complaint has been filed and then diverted to mediation, that complaint lies dormant, but may be reactivated if a resolution is not reached or if the resolution breaks down within a certain period of time. This use of sanction is analogous to social control in traditional communities, where a mediated settlement is a more pleasant alternative to retribution at the hands of the victim's extended family. People take mediation seriously if it means avoiding a less pleasant, less socially productive alternative; in the urban American case, the punitive alternative is the court. The threat of reverting back to court action also helps equalize status relations between parties because it gives the complainant a degree of social and punitive leverage that does not exist in the daily relations between individuals.

As mediation grows in scope within a community, it takes on a general community value as well. Disputes do not become public or the object of exaggerated neighbrohood gossip because confidentiality of the mediation proceedings are guaranteed to all disputants. But as mediation became an accepted alternative to court complaints, theory would predict a stronger neighborhood reaction to breached mediation settlements, even when the substantive issues of the particular dispute were not known.

Scarce Resources

The seventh principle of mediation is that *intangible social resources such as status, honor, prestige, and personal satisfaction are equal to or more important than tangible resources such as money, property, or land.* When people have simple monetary gains and losses to calculate in a dispute, mediation is a less successful form of resolution; the literature indicates that courts and the adjudicative process are widely and increasingly used to settle such claims, even in traditional communities (see Forman, 1972; Ruffini, 1978; Sarat, 1976; Todd, 1978; Witty, 1975, 1978; Yngvesson and Hennessey, 1975). In single-stranded relations, where moral obligation is not a salient feature of alliances, people tend to rank-order their priorities in favor of clear monetary gain. Even if shared community identity or the moral obligations of kinship are part of a personal relationship, a change in such relations is often signaled by a shift from emphasis on kinship to an emphasis on the transactional and situational nature of a particular dispute. Traditional and modern communities demonstrate remarkable similarity in this regard.

Right and Wrong

The eighth principle—that *reaching an agreement is more important than determining absolute right or wrong*—is corollary to the desire to settle in a conciliatory fashion in a nonpublic forum, and to the need to continue on-going interpersonal relationships. This principle further illustrates the future orientation of mediation; the resolution is less concerned with past events or precedents, and takes the transgression or disputed act as a given. The facts are important in assessing appropriate restitution, but they are less important than planning for the future of the social relationships involved in the dispute.

Participatory Agreements

Finally, there is the principle that *people are more likely to adhere to agreements they understand and have an integral part in making, than to agreements which are externally imposed.* This principle directly raises the question of legitimacy. For social institutions to work, legitimacy must be implicitly or explicitly derived from the community. If there is a crisis in legitimacy in which people feel powerless to control their own external lives and the bureaucratic institutions that regulate the external, sustaining environment (such as welfare departments, social security administrations, housing and urban renewal administrations, utility companies, the police, and the courts), people will lose faith in their social institutions and the law before they will lose faith in their social groups. If one subscribes to the large body of emergent literature that describes new political alliance formation along racial, ethnic, and occupational lines in urban areas, widespread alienation from government and local governmental administrative agencies, and a concurrent crisis in legitimacy around local court and law enforcement agencies, the argument that people are banding together locally in defiance or avoidance of government institutions is well grounded in over a decade of social science observations (Cahn and Cahn, 1964, 1966; Elias and Scotson, 1965; Moynihan, 1969; Packer, 1968; Task Force, 1967; Auerback, 1976; Beck, 1977; Black, 1973, 1976; Byles and Morris, 1977; Champagne, 1976; Curran and Spalding, 1974; Galanter, 1974, 1976; Lerner, 1979; Marks, 1971, 1976; Nader and Singer, 1976; Rabin, 1976; Stack, 1974;

Yin and Yates, 1975). The failure of individuals and communities to believe that state institutions can resolve, through expenditure and expertise, such problems as inflation, housing, welfare, crime, energy, justice, and dispute settlement raises the question of real alternatives to adjudication and decentralized community control at a time when social indicators show interest in community revival and struggle against individual powerlessness in American society (see also Nader et al., 1978).

Premises

The principles of mediation, and the theoretical propositions that follow, rest on two premises. Any analysis of the principles or the propositions of mediation without reference to these conceptual premises would be both inaccurate and incomplete.

First, *the principles need not be indigenous or preexistent in a social setting for mediation to be successful.* These principles are the critical variables that must be generated, or tapped into, for mediation to be a successful means of conflict management at the community level. The social and political milieu of a dispute is as important as the procedural style of the resolution to the long-range outcome. Without the participants' shared belief in these nine social and psychological principles, mediation practiced at its best will not work, or at the very least will not establish lasting solutions to interpersonal problems. This brings us to the second premise.

To some degree or another, *each of the principles involves the particular belief that certain factors exist or are important.* Whether they are analytically present, present in varying degrees, or even factually true is a secondary consideration in assessing the effectiveness of the mediation process. If people believe that avoiding the courts, finding a solution they can be happy with, expressing their personal frustrations, and living with a sense of local identity are important to their lives, then mediation will work for them, even if community identity or other variables are not present in statistically significant amounts.

Propositions

The theory of mediation in society rests on five propositions:

1. Mediation varies directly with the cumulative presence of the nine principles of mediation.
2. Mediation varies directly with political and cultural distance from the law.
3. Mediation varies inversely with social stratification.

4. Mediation varies directly with the presence, or wish for the presence, of on-going social relationships.
5. Mediation varies directly with the integration of the system of competitive resources in a system of reciprocal obliations.

First, *mediation varies directly with the cumulative presence of the nine principles of mediation.* The prevasiveness of each principle in the community and the number of principles that are operative in the community have a cumulative effect; the greater the quantitative intensity and number of principles in a community, the greater the probability of successful mediation.

Within this general social organizational guideline of predictive variables, there is a second proposition that *mediation varies directly with political and cultural distance from the law.* The greater the alienation and distance experienced by an individual or an entire community from the substance of legal institutions, the greater the possibility that mediation exists or could be implemented. Following from the discussion of the dual perspective among individuals in a culturally and ethnically plural society, the greater the incongruity between local and national cultural belief systems, the better the social conditions for local mediation and conciliatory types of settlements in general. The greater the congruity between the two belief systems, the greater the likelihood that mediation will not be the preferred form of dispute settlement.

This second proposition has two corollaries:

1. Mediation varies directly with the centralization and bureaucratization of law.
2. Mediation varies directly with autonomous and decentralized community identity and leadership patterns.

The more local dispute settlement and conflict management are centralized and pulled into an external governmental system, the greater the isolation of the individual from the principles and moral jurisdiction of the national legal system. This is particularly true if community authority and local leadership remains strong, viable, and legitimate within the community. As long as local elites, elders, landowners, or citizens have an interest in maintaining the autonomy of a local system that is responsive, mutually satisfying, understandable, and reciprocal, the separation from formal law continues to widen and deepen.

This proposition is similar to Black's (1976) theoretical discussion of the behavior of law in which he states that:

"Law varies inversely with other social control [p. 107]."

And,

"Law is greater in a direction toward less culture than toward more culture [p. 65]."

The first statement is supported by the pattern of urbanization and bureaucratization of western legal systems that has been previously noted, and the colonial and neocolonial experiences of traditional developing communities. The proposition that mediation will succeed the more people are distanced from the law is complementary of Black's (1976) restatement of the variables to note that the "law is stronger where other social control is weaker [p. 107]." As dispute settlement based on shared values, on-going relations, and a belief in egalitarianism decreases, formal governmental control in the form of law steadily increases. But alienation from the law simultaneously lessens its legitimacy and effective ability to bring satisfaction and resolution to peoples' personal and community problems.

Black's second statement diverges slightly in substance from the thrust of the mediation argument. Groups that differ in social status in a culturally plural political system do not have less culture than other groups, they have less power to control the movement of the legal system against them, less economic and political power to escape the legal process once enmeshed, and less power to use the law for their own benefit (see Cahn and Cahn, 1964, 1966; Auerbach, 1976; Galanter, 1974). Black uses the term *culture* as the equivalent of quantifiable educational and socioeconomic status. A person of more culture within this definition is a person at or near the center of the dominant, respectable, mainstream social group. It is this group that defines the dominant moral order and gives legitimacy to the bureaucratic institutions that arise to implement moral order. *Culture*, as used in the theory of mediation, covers a much wider range of rules, behaviors, ideas, and cognitive frameworks that a person learns in a particular way and passes on to subsequent generations; culture in this sense has a material and an emotional aspect. *Culture*, as used in this discussion, is synonymous to what Bateson (1936) has called ethos, or "the expression of a culturally standardized system of organization of instincts and emotions of the individuals [p. 118]." Culture in this widest sense encompasses both real observable behavior, rules, systems, ideas, material artifacts, and symbols, and the affect and meaning assigned to them. This definition of *culture* is a general anthropological one and is consistent with the belief and cognitive structure content discussed by Norton (1978) in her argument that the dual perspective arises from incongruities in such fundamental cultural components.

Black (1976) uses a narrower quantifiable measure of culture when he argues that "all else constant, an offense by someone with less culture than his victim is more serious than an offense in the opposite direction [p. 65]." This use of the term *culture* is similar to the use of the term *status* in this discussion, but in stating a relationship between law and quantifiable amounts of culture or status, Black pinpoints the behavior of law as it increases in quantitative amounts; it is this increase in law as a measurable attribute that ultimately leads to the favorable conditions for the persistence of or reinstitution of local mediation.

Law perpetuates powerlessness, racism, and anonymity within a community by reacting in differential fashion to stratification, social conventionality, presence or lack of quantifiable culture, and cultural differences. This separation of law from the social fabric of communities creates the cultural and political distance that prompts people to look back to themselves for control and organization.

These relationships between culture, status, and mediation are more succinctly stated as the third proposition—that *mediation varies inversely with social stratification*. The more equal the parties and the less differentiated the community in terms of status and economic power, the greater the viability of mediation. In socially and economically stratified communities, mediation *can* be successful, if egalitarian status markers are symbolically flexible. If, for the purposes of a conciliatory settlement, parties to a dispute can abide by the equality of status marked symbolically and fostered procedurally by mediation, even if such equality is seen by the parties as symbolic and highly situational, the mediation process can proceed to a successful conclusion.

Mediation will not work where economic or social status differences are extreme and the parties are not willing to set such differences aside for the sake of settlement. Thus, in cases of extreme differences in wealth, mediation will tend to give way to arbitration and adjudication in order to equalize the status of the parties with statutory obligations and protect the interests of the poorer or less-statused individual.

In rigid ordering of social class and status, such as the caste system in India, theory would predict that mediation between castes would be less likely than mediation within castes. Conciliatory agreements, however, can be obtained at the local level in highly stratified societies. Bailey (1960, 1965) has cogently described the conciliatory functioning of local village tribunals, or *panchayats*, in local Indian communities through the establishment of group consensus. In accordance with the corollary that mediation succeeds the more autonomous the local social organization and leadership, local needs and relations are likely to overcome most status barriers, whereas supralocal relations decrease the probability of such reciprocity taking precedence over transaction.

The importance of local-level social organization introduces the fourth proposition of mediation—that *mediation varies directly with the presence, or wish for the presence, of on-going social relationships*. The importance of continuity in relationships has been raised throughout the discussion of mediation. The cross-cultural evidence shows that people who interact reciprocally on a daily basis have a strong tendency to favor mediation because of the future social orientation of the conciliatory outcome. The degree to which interaction or the *wish* for interaction exists in any community is a restable variable, but one that cannot be discounted in urban American neighborhoods. American mediation programs show that the desire for the introduction of more personal interaction with one's neighbors is a real and active part of American urban existence (see Chapter 7).

Finally, there is the proposition that *mediation varies directly with the integration of the system of competitive resources in a system of reciprocal obligations.* The greater the degree of attachment of the system of competition over resources (especially scarce resources) to systems of reciprocal obligations such as kinship, patron–client relations, or political brokerage, the better the conditions for long-range, successful mediation. This proposition links local autonomy and leadership to the larger, external political organization within which communities exist. Barth (1959, 1963), Bailey (1971), Collier (1979), and others have discussed the integrative functions of local elites and political brokers in different culture areas (see Banton, 1965a; Befu, 1967; Blok, 1969, 1973, 1974; Boissevain, 1966, 1969b, 1974; Epstein, 1961, 1974; Frey, 1965; Geertz, 1963; Srinivas and Beteille, 1964; Gonzalez, 1973; Peters, 1977; Quandt, 1970; Roos and Roos, 1971; Salzman, 1974; Witty, 1975). Elites and brokers provide linkage between local, regional, and national power groups. Such leadership networks, which are both locally autonomous and externally connected, provide a reciprocal system of transactions and services that regulate local and supralocal allocation of resources. These resources may be tangible in the form of land, animals, water, or property, or intangible in the form of reputation, status, honor, and respect. The greater the range of influence of these brokerage and leadership networks, the more pervasive and strong mediation is likely to be because all competition systems are effectively functioning with a closed system of reciprocity and exchange. Haas (1971) has further noted the importance of such regional leadership networks to questions of national development and regional integration.

> Regional "subsystems" involve descriptions of the particularly intense interactions in a given locale... explained largely in terms of the inputs of the "system."... Regional subsystems, then, are devices for explaining the interdependence between local ties and concerns and the larger world which constrains them [p. 8].

Because of the social and regional integration that patronage and brokerage provides, the Middle East has very well-developed mediation systems. Every villager, no matter what his or her family rank or status, is internally supported by a regional elite, and externally connected to national political networks and institutions through the same individual. The operation of internal mediation and external intermediation, or influence bargaining, is discussed in Chapters 4 and 6.

Mediation will be a less favored form of dispute settlement if the elites have no interest in maintaining local patronage relations within the community, or if they remove themselves physically or psychologically from the affairs of the village and region. The active participation of brokers and elites will encourage contact and alliance between local residents and influential outsiders, and the subsequent development of open, individually competitive market systems linked to outside normative values. Elites can control such contact and communication with external political economic interests, however. Bailey (1969) has argued that the distinction between "insiders" and "outsiders", or "us" and "them" can be manipulated by political "middlemen" to foster misunderstanding and distrust, and Collier (1979) further notes that "elites may prevent undesired contact between their followers and outside officials by providing such responsive local services that nonelite community members feel little need to invoke outside aid [p. 322]." (See also Blok, 1969; Boissevain, 1966, 1969b; Cohen, A., 1965; Elias and Scotson, 1965; Fallers, 1964; Nader, 1965a, 1965b; du Boulay, 1974; Peters, 1977; Vinogradov, 1973; Waterbury, 1970.)

As long as local individuals and communities are effectively served by local mechanisms and network systems into the outside world, the need for perpetual social relations, goodwill, internal solidarity, and reciprocity will support and encourage mediation and intermediation systems.

Conclusions

The theory of mediation draws together the predictive analytical variables that account for the success or failure of community mediation. The theoretical propositions may be subject to modification as new ethnographic material emerges and as experience with mediation in diverse modern forms increases. The existing literature is quite consistent in rendering a clear picture of the relationship between law, mediation, and social organization, however. The discussion that follows sets forth two case studies of mediation in diverse settings. The Lebanese mediation material is extensive (Chapters 2 through 6), and gives a comprehensive analysis of one of the most highly developed mediation systems in the world. The American case of mediation (Chapter 7) is presented in a briefer, profile form; the American material is complete enough, however, to provide a comparison of the analytical variables as they are structured within the theory of mediation. The comparison of cases and procedures gives range and depth to the theoretical propositions, and illustrates the mediation principles with detailed and rich dispute settlement materials.

2
Setting

Shehaam is an agricultural village in the central Beqaa Valley of Lebanon. The total population in the village during the winter months (October to May) is 900. As is typical of Lebanese villages, however, this population increases to over 1200 during the summer months as individuals return to summer in their natal village. This summer influx reunites families and provides some extra labor in the villages both in the households and in the fields.

Women return to the village with their husbands if they are both natives of Shehaam. Frequently, women come to the village with only their children, if their husbands must remain in the city to work; in these cases, the men join their families on weekends. If a woman's husband is from another village, the couple will usually split their vacation time between two villages.

Although the men who summer in Shehaam initially arrive in the village to visit their families and friends, the men spend a large proportion of their time in the fields. Summer residents supplement the field labor force and the men often remain for weeks at a time in the small farm houses located in the fields a mile or two from the village. Women remain in the fields for a number of days, but they travel back and forth between village and fields more often than the men carrying messages, food, fresh clothes, and supplies.

Summer residence provides people with opportunities to visit and exchange information with neighboring villagers as well. Although people from different villages meet in local markets, shops, mills, and commercial centers, the summer's work provides ample time to renew old alliances, create new ones, and seek economic and political information from a variety of different sources. Since more personal contact occurs during these summer months, this is also a period when more disputes erupt between individuals; often arguments that develop during the winter are physically enacted when a minor confrontation occurs in the fields.

Production is organized around kinship relations and obligations. Work in the fields is allocated as the demands of the family land dictate. For families with little or no productive agricultural land, work is available for women and men on the land of neighbors or relatives. Payment for such labor is customarily through some combination of cash and produce.

Not all families in Shehaam own productive farm land, although all families own their home sites in the village. Families that do not own farm land either work on the land of relatives and neighbors during the harvest season, or seek other types of work outside the village in nearby towns. Such families may also raise donkeys and cows that they rent to others for farm work. Women also sell milk and make cheese from the cows, goats, or sheep that many families keep in small numbers. A few families who own tractors work for wages on a day-to-day basis, and a few individuals supplement family incomes by becoming teachers in the village school (14 people) or being butchers (2), shopkeepers (9), and auto mechanics (3).

Most people who own substantial amounts of productive agricultural land are members of the Christian community. Only one Moslem family owns substantial amounts of farm land. Over 70% of the agricultural land registered for Shehaam is owned by Christian families, although they comprise only slightly more than 50% of the total village population. There is a wide range of variation in the amounts of land owned, yet nearly all the Christian families work plots of land for subsistence and profit. In contrast, over 50% of the Moslem families must earn substantial parts of their total income working as skilled and unskilled laborers. The reasons for this unequal distribution of land are historical and based on the politics of land surveys, colonialism, land registration, and family alliances.

Water was supplied to Shehaam as part of a continuing national development program in 1968. The introduction of a piped water system has allowed small family vegetable gardens to spring up around the houses and enabled the planting of fruit trees that lend some shade and soil control to the parched hillside. Running water has also given increased freedom to the women of the village because they no longer have to make frequent trips to the nearby well.

Water is life in this dry, wind-blown land. The control of water resources within the village leads to many disputes and has various political implications. Water for irrigation in the fields outside the village is centrally controlled by the municipality (like a county administration), and although this control is sometimes abused, illegal use of irrigation water is infrequent.

Shehaam has a police station with eight policemen and a police chief in residence for its 900 permanent inhabitants. Shehaam's station also has jurisdiction over eight other small Shia Moslem villages in the surrounding areas. The village contains a government elementary school that draws teachers and pupils from all religious groups in Shehaam and other pupils from small neighboring villages. The school principal and most teachers (17 of 22) are village residents, but five male teachers are strangers to the village and find temporary housing with village families during the school year.

The village population is a mixed community of Shia Moslem, Greek Orthodox, Greek Catholic, and Maronite peoples. A census taken in the spring of 1973 revealed the religious affiliations presented in Table 2.1.

Households are composed primarily of nuclear families. Residence after marriage is typically in the husband's village or religious section, and frequently in his natal home, until the couple can afford to build a home of their own.

The early immigrants to Shehaam clustered according to religious affiliation. Gradually there developed geographically separate religious communities within the village. Religious communities still exist today and people continually refer to being "among the Shia" or "among the Maronites" when speaking of a specific location in the village. Villagers refer to the "upper" and "lower" village, thereby making a distinction between the more rigid religious divisions above and the mixed, random settlement patterns which have developed below. Though a Catholic would never build a new house in the old Maronite section of the upper

TABLE 2.1
Percentage of Village Population by Religion and Number of Households

Religion	Households (Percentage of N)	Individuals (Percentage of subtotal)	Total population (Percentage of N)
Shia Moslem	35	Men 23 Women 23 Children[a] 54	40
Maronite	29	Men 22 Women 22 Children 56	26
Greek Orthodox	21	Men 21 Women 27 Children 52	20
Greek Catholic	16	Men 21 Women 32 Children 47	14
	N = 136		N = 902

Source: Witty, 1978.
[a] Children = persons under 20 years of age.

village, such a house may easily be built between a Maronite and a Moslem on the land below.

Any village in Lebanon with over 50 inhabitants is entitled under the constitution to elect a mayor. Shehaam has two mayors, one for the Christian community and one for the Moslem community. Although the concept of village solidarity is very strong, villagers explain the existence of two mayors as a function of the large size of the village population; because the population is equally divided in number, they say, the two groups deserve to be equally represented to the outside world by two mayors.

As village representatives, the two mayors are active in local politics and in the mediation of disputes within the village and region. These combined activities serve to expand their system of personal, political, and economic alliances. The two mayors and the other elected official in Shehaam, the president of the municipality, are pivotal figures in local and regional political ritual and religious life. As respected public figures, they are often consulted by villagers in times of personal crisis, and their daily assistance in minor disputes, quarrels, and political tensions plays an important role in tempering violence and minimizing disputes among villagers.

Religious life in Shehaam is a matter of personal preference. Moslems may pray in their homes the prescribed three times daily, but many individuals do not perform the formal requisites of prayer or attendance at Friday mosque. *Ramadan* is the most important Moslem religious period, and fasting is observed dutifully by Moslem villagers during the entire month. The Prophet's Birthday is the second most important religious celebration. At this time special prayers are said in the mosque, the evening meal is a festive occasion with special dishes, and small sweet cakes are prepared by the women and distributed to the scores of friends who visit during the day.

In the village there is a Moslem *ulama*, or religious leader, who tends to the religious administration of the Moslem community leads prayers at Friday mosque, and advises individuals on religious matters. The *sheik*, as he is called locally, came to the village from Iran in 1972 to give the Moslem community religious counsel and guidance. He gave new impetus to the villagers' efforts to raise money for a *husseiniyya*, a social and religious center to be built near the village mosque.

Among Christians religious duties are also matters of personal preference and most individuals attend church regularly only for weddings and special religious holidays. Easter is the most important religious holiday for Christians; Easter is particularly festive in Shehaam because Orthodox Easter occurs 1 week after Catholic–Maronite Easter and tends to continue the festive feelings over a 2-week period. In addition, Easter is the appropriate occasion for settling family quarrels or ameliorating grudges between individuals. Christmas is the second most important religious holiday for Christians, and on this occasion there are

2. Setting

special midnight services in all three Christian churches. The Catholic and Greek Orthodox priests are residents of the village, but the Maronite congregation periodically brings in priests and bishops from the nearby Christian Market on a visiting basis; they have no priest in residence.

Agricultural life requires long hours of work during the productive seasons from April to November, and village life begins very early with the smell of coffee brewing in separate households long before sunrise. Before dawn the first tractors, cars, buses, and donkeys begin moving down the slope to the agricultural plains below, and the village comes to life. The gradual movement of people to the fields proceeds for most of the early morning hours. Later, groups of women can be seen setting off down the hill with baskets or sacks full of food and supplies as the noontime rest approaches. Other women are seen by midmorning on the roofs and porches of village houses chatting and playing with children, and a stranger to the place could easily fantasize about the relaxed pace of the farming life. In reality, the workday for women and men is 16 hours long with short periodic breaks throughout the day. Women who are drinking coffee and exchanging news and gossip at 10 A.M. have already completed 4 to 5 hours work by that time, and may have walked to the fields to perform some errands and returned.

Women work cooperatively with female relatives who live within shouting distance, and often other women friends from the larger support group are included in this work group, if they live nearby. The physical arrangement of individual houses, flat roofs, narrow streets, courtyards, and location on a graded hillside make for different size work groups among the women. The type of work performed affects the number who collect for work and morning coffee. Laundry is more of an individual or nuclear household task, while baking bread, making mattresses, or preparing wheat for storage are more likely to be larger joint work projects.

Agricultural produce is the livelihood and, villagers say, the strength of farmers of the Beqaa. For this reason, competition between families and within families is keen in the economic sphere. For a reasonable existence to be extracted from the land, long hours, plentiful rain, good weather, and judicious planning are required of each farming family. New and expanding opportunities in the schools and cities make a rising standard of living desirable, but the realities of weather, soil, and a precarious economy make it difficult to attain. Individuals often disagree as to the best way to maximize profits and family resources. This relation between the management of conflict, politics, and the family is the next subject that deserves our attention.

3
Family Organization: Tradition and Flexibility

Kinship and Community

Kinship and marriage ties are important to community life in Shehaam because situations involving conflict, authority, honor, and decision making begin with individuals, but focus on family groups. When people encounter various kinds of personal problems, strategies for resolution are situational and highly specific. Kinship and marriage ties constrain, and often define, the decision-making processes necessary for resolving each situation. The closeness of the kinship tie involved in a dispute and the seriousness of the case are the two primary factors that regulate problem solving and mediation within the community. Ties of kinship, friendship, and community are layered to form a series of concentric circles around each individual. These layers of affiliation and identity decrease in density in an outward direction; kin relations are denser than relations with non-kin neighbors and friends.[1] Every individual places every other individual conceptually on one point on her or his interconnected grid, so that each individual has a distinct social identity that must be dealt with very specifically.

This highly situational definition of social relationships is reflected linguisti-

[1]*Density* is a term derived from the analysis of social networks and refers to the frequency of personal interaction with each individual as well as within the network. Density refers specifically to the degree to which the individuals in one's personal network are themselves interconnected with one another. For a further discussion of network terminology, see Boissevain, 1974; Bott, 1957; and Mitchell, 1969.

cally. Villagers rarely use the pronoun *I*, but constantly refer to themselves and others in the plural form of *we*. The ubiquitous *we* in everyday speech refers to one layer of this concentrically expanding range of relationships; specific reference depends on the social context of the speakers.

Depending on the topic and audience, *we* could refer to the nuclear household, the extended family, one's primary or secondary religious affiliation, the entire village, or the regional community. In other words, *we* is a form of expression used situationally to refer to people in the family, those to whom the family is related through marriage, those who are potential marriage partners, and those with whom the family and village share common values and have long-standing relationships.

All individuals identify themselves within this progressively expanding range of social communities. Figure 3.1 illustrates the conceptual organization of these communities in Shehaam.

The Arabic word for "house" or "household" is *beyt*—the smallest unit of reference for what analytically is called the *nuclear family*. Family identity is a personal, ascribed status common to each villager and is his or her first source of social identity. The family unit is contained within the lineage and the clan. The clan is larger than the extended family and refers to all people descended from a common ancestor. Villagers use the term *family* to include all individuals in the lineage and clan, in a usage synonymous with what we would call the "family name"—Bakers, Millers, or Tylers. Within the clan there are subdivisions called *lineages*, and under special circumstances, such as a feud, the family reference may refer only to this lineage level of organization because the offending lineage within the clan is symbolically removed from alliances with the "family" until the rift has been repaired. But "family" to most villagers in normal situations is the identity associated with being a Hakiiim, a Maalouf, a Kazan, or a Rahman lineage member. Beyond the family, five other levels of identity are used to differentiate various levels of social distance (see Evans-Pritchard, 1940).

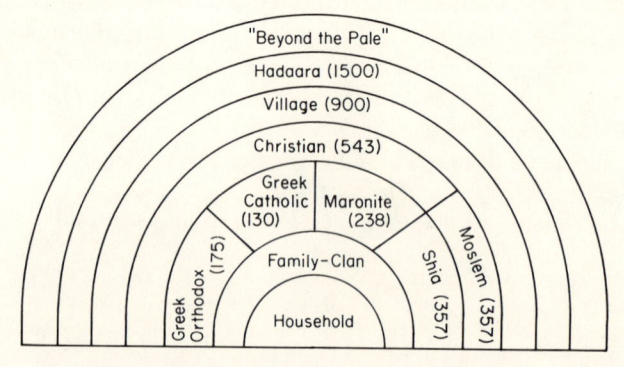

FIGURE 3.1. Types of self-defined communities.

The government is locally considered to be outside the household, family, religions, village, and regional community. Although the government and its various agencies contain indigenous Lebanese, "the government" as a structure is "beyond the pale" in the sense that it is considered to be the source of *external* order and authority within the regional community and village.

One's identity with a group is ideally derived from one's membership in a particular family, and then in a community. Women keep their natal family name even after marriage. While the family is important both in the villagers' conceptualizations of themselves and in formal interaction between individuals and groups, it is also a framework into which other types of ties are articulated. Kinship and marriage ties through both women and men create strategic links between individuals, families, and lineages. (See also Fortes, 1949, 1953; Barth, 1959, 1973; Leach, 1953; Murphy and Kasdan, 1959, 1967; Patai, 1955, 1965; Peters, 1960, 1963; Srinivas and Beteille, 1964.) Although the usual Middle-Eastern kinship discussion concentrates on descent reckoned through men and residence in the husband's home or village after marriage, the ties maintained through women in Shehaam lessen the exclusive importance of male-reckoned alliances, particularly with regard to political strategies and economic alliances.

The degree to which a family capitalizes on multiple types of linkages, such as female and male kinship relations, is a good indicator of political power, flexibility, and status within the village and region. While there is a strong tendency to marry within the village (90% for Moslems, 75% for Christians), relations outside the village are expanded through women as well as men. This does not mean, however, that men exchange their sisters in marriage outside the village simply to gain alliances with prestigious families in other areas, although this is one explanation for the function of such marriages, both in the Middle East and elsewhere (see Ayoub, 1959; Levi-Strauss, 1953; Patai, 1955, 1965; Chelhod, 1965; Cole, 1971, 1975). Women's ties to other families and their personal relations with other women can operate as pivotal links to successful managing of conflict, bargaining for influence, and generating political alliances. Without women's social and economic relationships, successful social and political maneuvering would be seriously circumscribed, if not impossible.

Marriage data from Shehaam indicate that women actively pursue marriage alliances outside the village on their own initiative if they sense the marriage will increase their own prestige and economic status and bring congruent status and support to their natal family and their offspring. Such alliances are usually made with specific economic and political consideration in mind. Women who have economic interests that they wish to maintain and women who wish to "rise out of the village" are women (usually under 25) actively seeking partners who will provide and/or encourage these goals. Given this type of strategy around a certain percentage of the marriages in the village, the role of women in cementing and strengthening their family's political and economic future should not be understated. Women operate all their lives within two distinct family groups, that of birth and that of marriage; these are two continually expanding family groups that women influence (see also Musil, 1928; Granquist, 1931; Ehrenfels, 1949; Dickson, 1951; Muhyi, 1959; Briggs, 1960; A. Fuller, 1961; Lutfiyya, 1966; Nevins, 1969; Dwyer, 1979; Fakhouri, 1972; Maher, 1974; Mernissi, 1975; Youssef, 1974).

Kinship in Everyday Living

An essential characteristic of all individuals in Shehaam, then, is that they not only have kinship links outside their families, but outside the village as well. These links mean that the number of alternatives for dealing with problems are greatly increased.

It is generally women who leave the village and live with their husbands upon marriage. The vast network of ties, male and female from her natal family, come with her to her husband's family. In this sense it is the women who bind the families of the area together, and it is this factor that gives women the power to enhance or cripple the political assets of her own lineage and the lineage of her residence after marriage. Women not only operate their own political structures, but also directly influence the formal modes of interaction and decision making among men. More importantly, they draw from their bilateral networks within the family, and specifically from the varied associations with women in the family, the power to ultimately determine the political viability of any given family and any given household.[2] An example will serve to illustrate this phenomenon.

Figures 3.2 depicts four families who are related through marriage. Most nonessential kin have been removed for clear analysis, so that this diagram is a skeleton of the total family structure. Although all family members are informally involved in political affairs, people rely on specific individuals and their ties with others when they need influence brought to bear on other individuals or groups. This is true both in personal problem solving, as illustrated in Figure 3.2, and the broader-based mediation process to be detailed in Chapter 4.

The individual who has initiated this conflict is Ali, from the Shehaam family. Ali is having a dispute with Abdul, a member of a Hermel family who is related to him through marriage. The dispute is outlined briefly in Case 1 because it is the nature of influence channels through families that is of direct concern, not the precise nature of the conflict itself.

---

[2]*Bilateral ties* refer to ties through both the male and female, that is, through the mother's and father's side of the family.

Kinship in Everyday Living

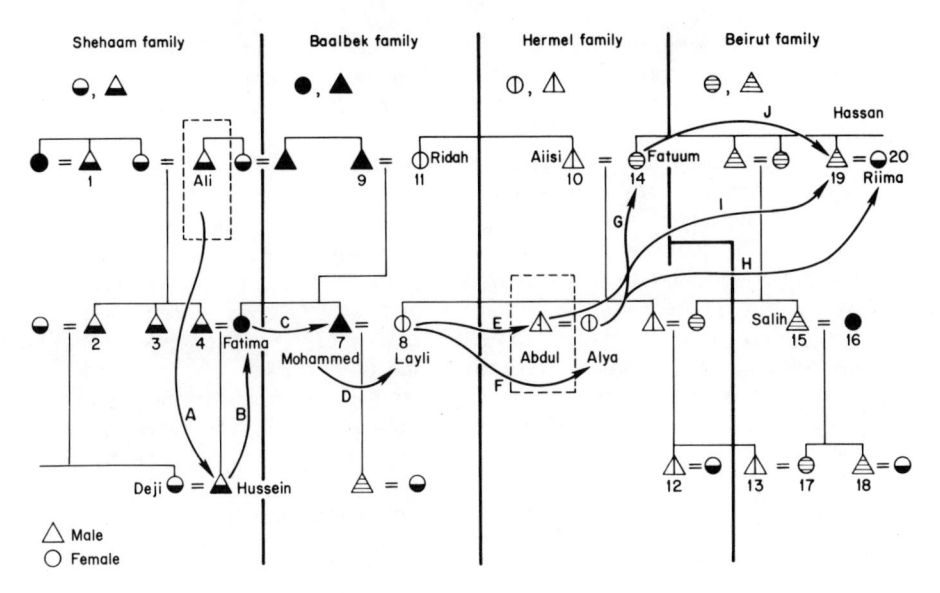

FIGURE 3.2. Interfamily action set.

CASE 1. THE CASE OF THE OLD STONE HOUSE

There is a piece of land in Hermel in which Ali, his grandson Hussein, and Abdul all hold portions of the title. On the land there was an old stone two-story house used primarily for storage of tools and equipment.

Abdul tore down this house to use the stone in a new construction nearby. When Ali and Hussein visited the area, the two older men argued, and a fight developed in which both men were slightly injured.

The problem that now faces Ali and his family in Shehaam is to reach and effectively influence a distant relative in Beirut; his name is Hassan (19, Figure 3.2). Hassan is a lawyer and works in the Palace of Justice. Abdul has filed a formal complaint against Ali for physical assault and property damage. Ali's grandson, Hussein, was also named in the complaint and has been taken into custody by the military court in Beirut because he is a member of the Lebanese army. The goal is to release Hussein from prison. The charges against him must be dropped by Abdul and approved by the courts before the two families can begin to effectively mediate a resolution to the incident. Ali needs to reach Hassan, with Abdul, to accomplish this goal quickly and informally.

The steps that are initiated by Ali are lettered in the order in which they were taken and are indicated by the arrows in Figure 3.2. Ali does not get along well with his daughter-in-law, Fatima, but is on good terms with his grandson, Hussein. It was Hussein (before he was imprisoned) and his wife,

Deji, who appealed to his mother to speak with her family in Baalbek. Because Fatima and her brother's wife, Layli, are good friends, the link is easily made. Layli and her husband, Mohammed, go to speak with Abdul and his wife.

On this occasion other men from the Shehaam family, Persons 1, 2, 3, and 4 accompany Layli and Mohammed from Baalbek to Hermel. While the men drink coffee and discuss the affair, Layli and Deji speak to Alya and convince her that she must speak with her mother (Fatuum) and her mother's brother's wife (Riima). Alya would be able to speak with that family, though they are miles apart, because she has given Hassan land and goats in return for the right of usufruct as long as she lives and she visits them frequently in Beirut in order to see the grandchildren (13, 17, and 18). While the women are talking with Alya, the men from the Shehaam family persuade Abdul to mediate the dispute with the family; this means that they may now proceed to reach Hassan at the court in order to get the charges dropped without a hearing.

After several hours of discussion, Alya agrees to intervene through Fatuum and Riima, and Abdul concedes and agrees to speak with his father, Aiisi, about the dispute.

The next day the entire party makes the journey to Beirut (Persons 1–4, Mohammed, Persons 7–11, and 14). Ridah (11) is included on this trip as a respected and elder spokeswoman. Ridah's advice is also authoritative and supportive in this particular case, for she is Aissi's elder sister.

The group is lucky to find Hassan at home, and after many hours of coffee, cigarettes, and discussion, Hassan goes off to the courthouse to prepare for Hussein's release, accompanied by Ali and Abdul. The specific objective has been achieved. Once the problem has been solved except for the technicalities, conversation at Hassen's home turns to informal family business and local news, and the relatives settle in for a visit of several days.

The salient points in this example are (*a*) the various combinations of marriage ties and relations through both women and men that are operationalized, and (*b*) the fact that in order to influence a man, efforts are simultaneously made to contact and influence his wife.

The relationships between the women in this case are complex. As noted, women have a sphere of power and authority separate from the men's. If flexibility in reaching allies is to be maintained, women and men must work together, as this example illustrates, to combine their spheres of influence in order to achieve a particular goal. The major players in this particular case indicated that an important factor in making the choices within the parameters of kinship and marriage is not necessarily the directness of the kinship ties involved, but the selection of supportive versus unsupportive ties at any given time. The situational aspect of a support network is critical in a conflict. Only the kin who are also part of one's effective support network are eager to give effective assistance. Kin who are temporarily or permanently alienated from one's network are avoided if possible. For this reason, Persons 15 and 16 were not contacted, and did not accompany the entourage to Hassan's household. Although both 15 and 16 have direct family ties to the target couple, Hassan and Riima, relations between them are not cordial, for Salih (15) and Hassan were also disputing at the time of this action.

It is clear from this example that marriage ties through women are mobilized if they are present and effective. In this case, the link through a woman, Fatuum, was effective in bypassing a direct male link through Salih and his wife. As Abdul stated: "Of course, I will go to Hassan to ask his help, for he is obliged to me through marriage; my brother is married to his brother's daughter. But my mother-in-law is a strong woman and knows him well. My wife is more able to influence her and argue in my behalf, so that in this case it is important that she goes with us on our side. By this [action] Hassan also knows we do not try anything devious or unfair."

Factions and Kinship

It would be an oversimplification to say that family groups are synonymous with political groups. Factions exist within families and may be potentially splintered off by anyone in a household. Women do not initiate factional divisions within the family unit as frequently as men, but they are always instrumental in determining the character of factional alliance, the intensity and duration of conflict, and the maintenance of competiton. Men and women coordinate their political efforts in factional alliances and co-participate in the broad range of daily behavior, boundary maintenance, and social strategies that are an integral part of factionalized political activity. Women compete and maneuver within political structures of their own, however, and in this sense have factional alliances of their own, in the world of women, which overlap with those of the family. Frequently a woman's personal support alliances coincide with those in the family, but often they are separate networks of influence that can combine with, work in opposition to, or remain neutral to male political networks.

As noted, the women make and sell dairy products in the village and outlying region. In the course of this activity they perpetually travel and establish social and economic ties wherever possible.

Political competition between women is not peripheral to general social life. In one particular situation when men from two families agreed that one could use the other's black goat-hair tent for a party and feast, women from the borrowing family refused to allow this transaction to take place. Their refusal was based on fierce economic competition between the women of the two families and

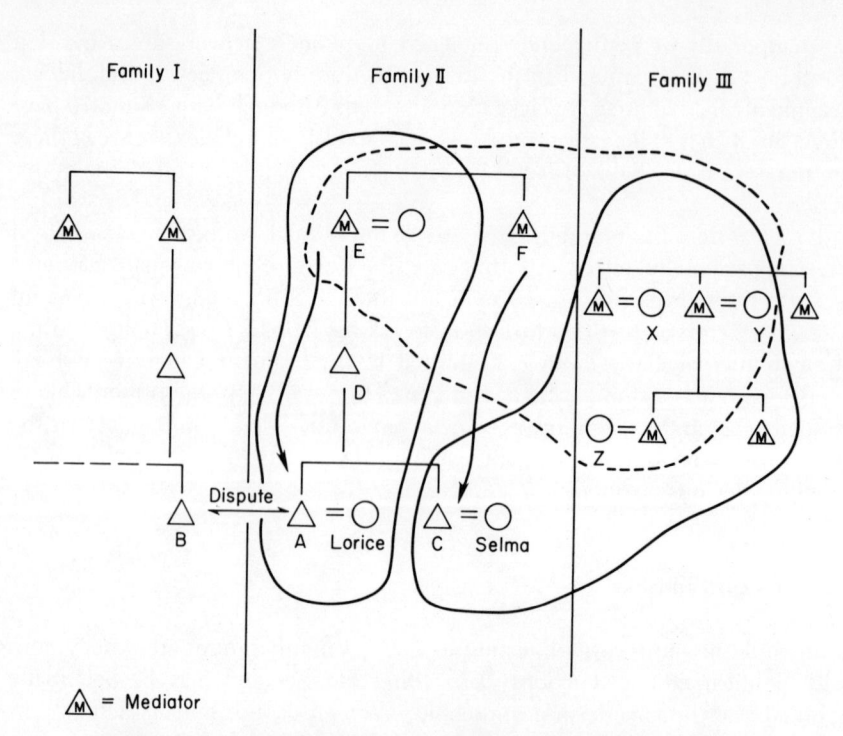

FIGURE 3.3. Interfamily factional divisions. (Source: Witty, 1978.)

disagreement over client routes and purchasing agreements. Here, the women's goals and strategies were contradictory to the men's, and their interests prevailed in this case because the contractual alliance between the men was tentative and new, while competition between the women was long-term and entrenched.

Factional divisions may occur within a family and divide what were once traditional allies. A typical division and its origins is diagrammed in Figure 3.3.

The family groups illustrated in Figure 3.3 depict a gradual shift in alliance and authority over time. The large dotted loop represents a factional alignment that existed several years before the present dispute; the alignment had been disbanded once the original goal had been achieved. One of the parties to this dispute (F) still remains friends with those members of Family III pictured in Figure 3.3. Then a dispute occurs (Case 2).

CASE 2. A CASE OF FACTIONAL INSULT

Persons A and B had a verbal argument and a physical fight, although no serious injury was sustained by either party. A's father began to press him

Factions and Kinship

almost immediately after the incident to settle the argument that evening. A's brother, C, however, argued against this action and was supported in his arguments initially by Persons E and F, his paternal grandfather and his grandfather's brother. All persons involved in this dispute, with the exception of B, were members of the same patrilineage.

Persons A, B, and C had been sharing farm labor and equipment when the fight between A and B occurred, but in the days that followed, C became irritated with his brother (A) and his father (D) because of their refusal to demand an apology from B, who had initiated the argument and insulted the family name.

The mediators in this case were elders from Families I, II, and III, indicated by M. Although this dispute was mediated and resolved, it created a permanent rift within Family II. Person C publically withdrew his support from his father's house, and with his grandfather's brother's (F) advice, began sharing labor and farm equipment with the persons indicated from Family III.

This shift occurred over a strong verbal protest from Persons A and D, supported by E, who wished to hold the family together at almost any cost. But because A, D, and E deeply distrusted those individuals in Family III and suspected that they had stolen some of their best crops during the previous 2 years, the opposition finally split Family II into conflicting groups indicated in the diagram by the solid line loops.

The authority for formal decisions now runs in two channels within this family: From E → D → A, and from F → C, as indicated by the arrows. A subsequent minor dispute between Persons A and F required mediation involving neutral, nonfamily mediators, an occurrence that would not have been necessary if the channels of influence and authority within the family had remained intact.

This internal family fragmentation cannot be completely understood by focusing solely on the precipitating dispute between A and B or on the opposition between the elder family patriarchs (E and F). Disagreements between brothers and cousins occur frequently, but are usually mediated within the family and do not lead to such serious oppositions as depicted in this example.

The women of this familial configuration played an integral part in the eventual outcome. C's wife, Selma, because of her education and because she is not native to Shehaam, is closely associated with the women of Family III (X, Y, and Z). This association is not only in terms of social compatibility and cooperative household activity, but also in areas of child-rearing and interests outside the household. Selma wants her children to be well-educated and able to leave the village if they wish. To this end she has gone into economic partnership with the women from Family III in a joint venture to sell milk and cheese throughout the area. Person E, her husband's grandfather, disapproves of this activity. Selma, as a result, stands in direct opposition to E's authority over her husband. She also dislikes the women related to and allied with A's wife, Lorice. Although it is not proper for Selma to oppose her husband's partrilateral elders directly, her economic ventures and her opposition to A's wife are a reality of the daily routine.

Thus, Selma and F are in agreement when A disputes with B. It is Selma and F who eventually persuade Selma's husband, C, that A did not take proper action against the insult to the family name. These arguments, plus support from a patrilineal elder (F), and a desire to continue Selma's economic ventures in cooperation with Family III, make the division between siblings a gradual reality, especially from C's point of view.

This conflict serves to illustrate how traditional values of achieved leadership, status, respect, and authority act as constraints upon individual action. In this particular case, Person C was greatly influenced in his choice of allies in an economic dispute by his patrilineal relative, F, and by his wife. Because F was well-known and respected, he was an elder of position and stature. This, combined with his aggressive personality, not only worked in this case to influence and counsel C, but also to alienate his own brother, E.

Although E had previously been allied with F in the economic activities of several years ago, in this case he abandoned those ties entirely and worked to influence A, directly and through an intermediary, D. He was strongly motivated by the insult to the family name that had been incurred by B during the argument with A, but also by jealousy of his younger, but well-respected brother (F). Person E used the argument for family honor and solidarity as a strong local traditional value in an attempt to outweigh the respect and strength of F. The result was to divide the family unit politically.

Although the precipitating dispute occurred in the third generation, between Persons A and B, the polarization of the family members can only be fully understood through consideration of several generations, and by considering the political alliances of all members of the participating households. If the complex, shifting relationships through time were not considered in this case, for example, one might incorrectly conclude that the economic dispute between A and B caused the split within Family II. Such a focus would also eliminate the influence of women in the village political system and strengthen the belief that only men are involved in political rivalry and competition.

Networks and Continuity through Kinship

Personal relationships between individuals and the relative weight of kinship obligations determine the effectiveness of personal networks. There are two main points to consider in assessing the characteristics of the political nature of kinship and non-kinship affiliations.

First, it has been shown that personal support networks are not replicas of kinship relations although support relationships within the family are usually quite dense. Relationships with relatives form the core of a person's support network, and such relationships are characterized by a strong degree of reciprocity and moral obligation.

Second, the dense family relations of one's personal care contrast with highly individualized and situational links to individuals in other families. Outside of the family, ties to individuals are based on a single transaction for a particular gain. In transactions observed in several support networks in Shehaam, interactions with the peripheral, nonfamily members of one's network was governed by the principle that the relationships do not continue as a matter of obligation and conscience, but only as a temporary commitment around a specified issue or goal. These ties to non-kin are peripheral in the sense that they reach outside the dense family core, to other social and geographical areas of the network (see Baily, 1969; Barth, 1963; Boissevain, 1974).

Individuals aligned voluntarily in this way are not morally obligated to one another through kinship to maintain a permanent, reciprocal bond of support. This does not mean that some core relationships do not involve transactions from time to time; but in the core, the reciprocal obligations are combined with the transactional elements, not in opposition to them. Thus, when issue-oriented alliance occurs within the family core, the basis for interaction and support is one of conscience and moral obligations *combined* with the perceived maximization of personal gain. Voluntary, calculated transactional alliances with non-kin often cross-cut religious boundaries. This adds both flexibility and depth to alliance building, and introduces uncertainty into the process of political resource gathering. One must constantly be working to keep kin ties strong, expand ties into other communities, and build diversity into non-kin ties. Such vigilance is necessary to maintain strong, interconnected personal networks. A constant realignment of non-kin allies is necessary so that severing one nonfamily tie will not sever connections to political allies and isolate a person completely from all of her or his nonfamily allies in the village.

Political success and status within the community is measured largely by the ability to mobilize and redesign diverse numbers of individuals. To do this effectively, one must have direct, person-to-person relations with people in different groups. The number of family ties relative to the number of transactional ties with nonfamily allies is an important ratio in determining the degree to which an individual can be isolated from supporters. Support networks with a mix of family and nonfamily links are much harder to weaken and break, especially if those networks span across all religious communities in the village.

A person's ability to succeed and maintain allies within the village is a mixture of skill, family relations, and personal initiative. The individuals pressing hardest for change within their family and village are the individuals who have the highest mixture of family and nonfamily alliances in their support networks. Those who are not pushing for change as rapidly have more inward-directed, family-based support networks.

Support networks are intertwined throughout disputing and mediation. The relationship of personal interaction, family, and community cohesion to dispute settlement within this larger system of competition is the next topic of discussion. Given the texture of family life and community organization that has been outlined for Shehaam, we will now explore the relationship between the traditional but changing family structures, and the various modes of settling interpersonal disputes.

4

Conflict Management and Dispute Settlement: The Mediation Process

Social Indicators: Status and Legitimacy

Villagers in Shehaam deal with conflict in a variety of ways. Although some of the local settlement strategies are also used with outsiders, villagers make procedural distinctions between disputes with "insiders" and "outsiders." This chapter will focus on "inside" disputes among villagers and subsequent chapters will discuss "outside" disputes.

It is necessary to first say a few words about the status indicators that influence the definition of who may be a mediator, and what community values are relevant in defining respectable behavior and norms.

Ideally, status and authority can accrue to all adults. Authority is exercised by men daily within the household, in political debates and gossip in the village, and through economic relationships with coworkers, kin, laborers, and shopkeepers. Women also achieve high status and exercise authority over the individuals within and beyond the household. Although men symbolically hold the ultimate authority for decisions, both women and men compete for status and the concomitant authority. Status can be thought of as existing in two separate spheres (female and male) that overlap one another. A woman's status among other women is maintained by her own personality, alliances, and behavior, and by the relative statuses of her families of birth and marriage. Likewise, a man's status is a function of his lineage membership, personality, and his political and economic astuteness. Ranking is worked out in relation to other men with whom he is in contact. These separate status systems are analogous to the separate competitive political spheres that were discussed in Chapter 3.

Age is the most important criterion of status for both women and men. Accumulated experience, knowledge of family histories, recollection of previous incidents, and a knowledge of local precedents are all attributes that the elder person actively contributes to social and political life as well as the management of conflict.

Marriage and the responsibility of a family also contribute to one's status in the community. Unmarried men over 30 are able to demand respect only from those who have less status (for example, unmarried girls, female age mates, children), but those same men gain a considerable amount of respect upon marriage and establishment of their own households. Marriage as a social indicator functions in the same manner for women. An unmarried woman, even if she is 60 years old, is still referred to as a "girl" in everyday conversation. This linguistic label does not change to "woman" until after marriage. No such language distinction is made for men. Women of mature age who have successfully raised families command a great deal of respect from younger persons, male or female, and depending on their political strength and cleverness, are able to maintain positions of status and political importance both within the family and the region.

As a personal characteristic, generosity is also important; people must be willing to give financial assistance to relatives and neighbors when they are able, without necessarily being asked. When support is actively requested, however, people should give of themselves as well as their wealth.

The ability to temper wealth with age, experience, and generosity is an important aspect of status, although the influence of wealth cannot be disregarded. A wealthy family is rarely considered of low status, but a poor family may have very high status on the basis of the personal attributes described previously. Villagers recognize that ideals such as generosity are conditional and constantly need to be reconciled with the competition and uncertainty that are realities of agricultural life.

Another status marker for elders and mediators are family ties to the regional community. It is within the boundaries of the regional community that authority, values, and status derive legitimacy (see Figure 3.1). This regional community is not a finite, bounded geographic area, but a conceptualization by the villagers of a cultural area in which the same values are shared and where personal relationships are of a long-standing and respected nature (see Wolf, 1966). A respected person must first be a person from the regional community. This usually means a native-born person, but with the high rate of emigration abroad and the subsequent return of children with various nationalities, the family origin rather than the actual place of birth is the functional criterion for determining a "child of the village" or "a child of the place." It is understood that if one is indigenous to the community, the customary practice, the kinship, and the history of the area are understood and accepted. These shared values, vil-

Social Indicators: Status and Legitimacy

lagers say, confer respect and prestige to community members. Such respect must be further justified through behavior, but the common basis for accepted norms rests in the community.

These concepts of community, family, respect, and honor underlie the entire mediation process. Whenever difficulties arise with an individual's willingness to accept any stage of mediation, these concepts will be invoked by the family or mediators. By appealing to higher moral standards, the bargaining for compromise and consensus is usually achieved. The actual payment, apology, sanction, or any other facet of the mediation process can also be influenced in the same manner.

A male elder tells the story of two men related through marriage in a neighboring village who were engaged in a series of arguments over a relatively small amount of money ($24) that one owed the other. Finally, after a particularly violent incident when one man struck the other with a chair, the injured man's paternal uncle went that same day and paid the debt for his kinsman. The injured party was humiliated by this act because his close relative had shamed him by paying a debt that he could have easily paid for himself if he had not persisted in being stubborn. His relative had taken action not only to keep an explosive situation from escalating, but also to strengthen family honor, and thereby show his nephew that he had been wrong. In this case, the shamed debtor later repaid his uncle the full amount.

In this manner, principles, higher priorities, and cultural ideals can be used to limit volatile behavior from within the group and prove in practice to be fairly effective mechanisms of social control.

Villagers believe that conflicts should begin and end within the community. It is also believed that families, more than individuals, are more aware of the history of family groups, economic ties, and kinship in the community. The family, they say, is aware of the overall importance of dignity and nobility in dealing with others. Although these ideals may be forgotten by an individual in times of anger, time and people work together to reintegrate and realign the values of the village.

It is crucial that mediators be respected elders. In this way, mediators provide an organization for leadership and social control within the community. The characteristics of status make a man better able to consider disputes in a long-term perspective and weigh the wealth of historical evidence that enters into most mediation discussions. Furthermore, because mediation functions to reaffirm the integrity and honor of the disputing families, selecting a nonrespected mediator would be a serious insult to all the participants. A man under 40 is rarely considered respected within the limited context of mediation, although he may be highly "respectable" in general village affairs and an asset and pride to his family.

Leadership

THE MAYOR

Some individuals, because of their experience and reputation, are routinely involved in mediation. The mayor (*mukhtaar*) is one such individual. Informants agree that the political role of the local mayor was much more important and powerful before independence than it is today. The mayor is a 4-year elected official, but the position is usually held for consecutive terms and is not relinquished until the incumbent tires of the administrative duties involved or is ousted by a rival faction. Shehaam has two mayors, one Moslem and one Christian.

Officially, each mayor gives administrative sanction to marriages. In the same official fashion, he records births and deaths within his community.

Although the position of mayor is formally administrative, it holds a great deal of prestige and influence within the village. One of the most influential aspects of this position is that the mayors are always involved in mediation in surrounding villages when regional participation is required (see page 30). Many respected men in Shehaam are periodically involved in these regional settlements, but each mayor is officially the nucleus of a conciliatory group from his religious community in Shehaam.

As a powerful and influential male elder, each mayor is actively involved in the peace-keeping and mediation procedures within the village. In disputes between Christians and Moslems, the two mayors work together gathering information and acting as mediators in conjunction with family elders to insure that such cross-community conflict does not escalate.

Unless a dispute involves the mayor directly, he is usually involved in a conciliatory capacity in a wide range of family and community disputes. He is also often brought into minor disputes, quarrels, property thefts, minor property damage, and stolen animal cases that occur within the village. For most villagers, their mayor is an influential and relatively neutral third party who can advise, calm, and often settle problems directly. A mayor will often undertake quiet investigations, asking questions throughout the village, and consulting privately with appropriate families. In this way a mayor often acts to minimize the hostilities that flare up between individuals and factions by quietly resolving the tensions and minor disputes occurring between villagers. Case 3 will serve to illustrate the activities of the mayor in such a minor incident.

CASE 3. THE CASE OF THE STOLEN BOX

Rachad N. is a Greek Orthodox man from Shehaam. Upon returning from a visit in Beirut, he found that his home had been broken into and that a

Leadership

box containing some clothes, money, gold pieces, and several sentimental family objects was missing. Rachad went that evening to the home of the mayor (Christian) and told him of the loss. He felt that he knew who was responsible for the theft but hated to cause an incident.

The mayor, Elias, told him not to worry, but to go home and wait. Elias promised that he would make some personal inquiries of his own.

About a week later, Elias appeared at Rachad's home, carrying the missing box. Following Rachad's suspicions and his own intuitions. Elias had located the thieves and pressured them to return the box, no questions asked. The threat Elias had used against them was open dispute and the possible intervention of the police in the incident.

Rachad asked whether his suspicions were correct in the case, but Elias replied that the box and its contents were safe and accounted for, and that this should be the end of the matter.

In this case, the mayor successfully initiated a personal inquiry, recovered the stolen property, and minimized tensions and suspicion. The exact methods used or the network of people involved is unknown in this case, but Case 4 illustrates in more detail a typical set of procedures for investigating a provocative incident.

CASE 4. THE CASE OF THE STOLEN SHEEP

Early one morning it was discovered at the house of Abraham in the upper village (a Maronite), that one of his sheep was missing. He insisted that they had all been present the night before.

There was some discussion with his brother next door. They decided to have breakfast and coffee and then go out and do some questioning to see if anyone had seen or heard anything during the night. One of the children was dispatched to inform the mayor, Elias, and after coffee he and his oldest daughter arrived at Abraham's house; Abraham and his brother recounted the story, and the entire group set out together to investigate.

The neighbors had not heard or seen anything, although they had been sleeping on the roof. The visiting group had coffee there. Abraham was asked if he was sure the sheep could not have just wandered out; he replied no, that was not possible.

Next the group proceeded up the hill to the house of Moussi, a Moslem, which stands directly above Abraham's on the hillside. He also had heard nothing, but promised he would see what he could find out on his own.

The group then proceeded further up the hillside to the house of Butros, another Maronite. He was not at home, so Elias told his wife the situation and asked her if she had seen the sheep, or heard any strange noises during the night. Again the reply was negative, but she promised to tell Butros when he returned from the fields.

The group was still standing in front of Butros' house debating where to proceed, when Elias' youngest son came to tell him that Subhi was waiting for him at home. Elias and his daughter returned to the house, and Abraham and his brother went to visit a nearby neighbor.

Subhi, a Moslem, had been negotiating with Abraham to buy some 15–20 sheep for several days. Subhi was surprised that Abraham had not returned with Elias, and the young boy was dispatched to bring him to the house.

There was some general conversation about work in the fields, the crops, how much each thought they might yield this season, and how other people's crops were doing. Coffee was made.

Subhi lit a cigarette and said that he had heard that Abraham was looking for a lost sheep. Elias said yes, that was true, and briefly related the morning's events.

Subhi then said that he might know something of the incident; he had come across one of his young relatives on the road this morning with blood on his clothes and carrying a knife in his belt. He had asked him what he was doing coming towards the village so early in the morning (5 A.M.), and why he had bloodstains on his clothes.

At this point in the conversation Abraham arrived and drank coffee, while Elias retold Subhi's story to him. Subhi suggested that they go and ask the boy's father about the incident this evening (he was in the fields now). He requested that he not be mentioned by name, but that he felt it was necessary to the relations between the families that these incidents be cleared up as soon as possible. He gave a brief description of the boy as being rather impulsive and irresponsible, which is why his father refuses to send him to school. The boy stays at home causing trouble, and he refuses to go and work in the fields although he is 17 years old. Elias and Abraham both thanked him for coming, and said they would do nothing until they talked to the boy and his father that evening.

After he had gone, they discussed his story briefly, asking what the other thought of it. Abraham thought Subhi was worried about an argument arising between them because he wanted to buy his sheep, and thought, therefore, that the story was probably true. Elias said he would go to see the boy's father that evening and see what he could find out.

That evening about 7 P.M., Abraham arrived at Elias's house, and Elias's youngest son was sent to see if Aziz (the suspect's father) was home. The message came that he had just returned, so Abraham, Elias, and his eldest son, Joseph, walked through the village to Aziz' home.

Aziz was just finishing washing his feet in a bowl in the sitting room, and motioned for the group to come in. He wiped his hands with a towel, and then greeted the visitors and asked them to sit down. Pillows were arranged comfortably on the floor by the eldest daughter, and ashtrays and cigarettes were brought by the younger children.

Aziz settled himself, lit a cigarette, and said that they must eat with them, as his wife was preparing dinner now and they would eat soon.

Leadership

Elias asked Aziz how his fields and crops were progressing and this discussion lasted for some time. Aziz then asked Joseph if his wife had given birth yet, and he replied that she had not, although it was time. The conversation continued in this social vein for another 10 minutes or so. Then the coffee that had been heating over charcoal was brought in and served by the host. While the coffee was being poured and enjoyed, Abraham stated that this morning he had discovered a sheep was missing, and that they had come to ask him about it because they felt that he or his son could help them solve this problem. Aziz asked in what way.

Elias then related how his son had been seen outside the village this morning very early with a knife in his belt and blood on his shirt. He did not mention Subhi by name, or even mention that it had been said by a relative.

Aziz called to the other room for his wife, and when she appeared, he asked where the boy was. She said he had been there earlier in the afternoon, but was now out and she did not know where. Aziz then dispatched a younger boy to check at the houses of his brother's friends and find him and bring him home.

Aziz then said that they would see what his son had to say. He himself had been in the fields all day, and had not seen his son since the day before. He said he did not see why his son would have any reason to steal a sheep from Abraham. Elias replied that they did not know either, and conversation continued to focus on farming.

The son, Abdul, finally arrived about one-half an hour later. His father began the questions by asking him where he had been so early this morning and why he had been out of the village. The boy replied that he could not sleep so had gone to look for firewood. Aziz countered with the fact that his wife had told him that Abdul was not in the house at all when the rest of the family went to bed at 10:30 P.M. (Aziz had not been there; he had slept in the fields.) Aziz then changed the subject and asked to see the clothes Abdul had been wearing that morning. He asked him why he had changed. The young man was trying to look very bored; he sauntered out and brought back some black slacks and a brown shirt that had stains on the sleeves. He did not know where the stains came from.

At this point Aziz got angry and cuffed him on the side of the head and told him to wait for him in another room. He took several minutes to calm down; Abraham lit another cigarette, and everyone sat without speaking. Then Aziz said he was not convinced that his son was guilty of anything, but that he would talk with him privately, and then talk with them again.

Elias said that this would be fine, that they did not like to intrude on family matters, and that they should discuss the matter within the family. The visiting group rose and quietly left.

Two weeks later, Aziz, his uncle, the Moslem mayor, and another Moslem elder arrived at Abraham's house around 8 P.M. A boy was sent next door to summon Elias who had been informally informed of the impending visit, and he arrived when coffee was being served. Unlike the previous evening, everyone this evening knew what the subject was, and came directly to the point.

Aziz's uncle pointed out that they, the family, had been discussing the matter of the stolen or lost sheep. Both of their sons said they were not involved, but say it was someone else from the family. Whether the fathers believed this story, or whether it was true was never stated, but the mayor said that they would rather compensate Abraham now for the sheep, and find out later who was involved. They are fairly certain it was more than one person, and it seems they may all be lying to protect one another. He felt confident that they would find out the entire story in the end, but for the sake of peace and the family name, they wanted this evening to settle with Abraham for the price of the sheep.

Abraham agreed to that, and Elias agreed with a headshake, but added that he certainly expected no repeat of this type of incident. The other mayor assured him that the boys, whoever they were, would be dealt with.

The question remained of how much payment was expected for the sheep. Abraham stated that he had talked to a buyer several weeks before, and was promised 70 LL (approximately $24) per head. There was some discussion about this: Was the sheep large or small, how fat was it? nobody was sure. There was a silence, more coffee drinking, more cigarettes lit, and everyone sat for a few moments, thinking. Finally, Elias suggested that they look at the remaining flock to get an idea of the size.

Everyone adjourned outside and inspected the sheep. Aziz offered to pay 60 LL on the spot after inspecting several sheep. Everyone went back into the house. The Moslem mayor then asked Elias what he thought. He said that Abraham's previous buyer had included ewes and rams and such differences in size in his price, and that 70 LL was a fair price as they were all relatively the same size. Aziz reached a decision at this point, and spoke briefly with his uncle. He said that they would pay the 70 LL. The money was produced between the two of them, and handed to Abraham. He thanked them.

There was a momentary silence, and then Elias said that such incidents really must be stopped for the good of everyone, and made a few remarks along those lines. Coffee was brought out and they all drank, the guests served first. Shortly after, they departed.

A number of factors that are important conflict resolutions in Shehaam appear in this case. Villagers say that the family is a unit where arguments should ideally be resolved in privacy. However, family members may break ties of rigid loyalty if other types of alliances, particularly economic ones, take precedence. Thus Subhi's offering of information against a relative in a minor incident was prompted by his future economic alliance with Abraham.

Both mayors frequently function as mediators and intermediators speaking on behalf of other parties, exerting social pressure, or tempering violence. This role is critically important. An injured party is willing to wait days or weeks because she or he knows that a resolution is in process. The outcome is a higher priority than the "truth" about a particular incident; this is particularly true when personal injury is not an issue for compensation.

Minor incidents are frequent and much of the mayors' time is spent soothing feelings, applying an even hand, listening to complaints, and clarifying facts. The procedures they use require that they know a great deal about family history, personalities, business relations between villagers, kinship ties, and general history of the area.

Each mayor, as we have seen, plays an important role in this investigative procedure. Furthermore, the police cannot officially enter or search any house in the village without the presence of the appropriate mayor. This practice involves him in many disputes. His role is only limited by the degree to which the case is sensitive to the factional organizations which cross-cut the community. The mayor's presence generally adds weight and validity to an investigation because it adds a degree of formality to the proceedings. Villagers solicit the service of the mayor associated with their own religious community: Moslems go to the Moslem mayor, Christians to the Christian mayor. If a Christian should have a complaint against a Moslem, she or he collects several relatives, and together with the Christian mayor, they go to the home of the Moslem mayor and present the situation. Then the Moslem family is consulted by the group.

In this way, the mayors function as intermediaries between the two primary religious groups in the village, particularly if two disputing families have no social or economic relationship. If a relationship exists between any families in conflict, the male elders of the family will usually attempt to resolve the dispute personally before calling in the mayor and other male elder leadership. The presence of both mayors at all Christian-Moslem mediations, weddings, funerals, and other public events also serves to formally acknowledge the juxtaposition and integration of Christian and Moslem values and interests within the village.

PRESIDENT OF THE MUNICIPALITY

The only other elected official in the village is the president of the municipality, elected for a period of 6 years. The president's range of influence is expanded in the same manner as that of the local mayors. He has authority over decisions regarding the allocation of municipal funds and individuals are constantly trying to influence him to release money for special projects that they would like to see completed in the village. Such favors would include paving the road or supplying new electrical lighting in certain parts of the village.

The president plays another important role in village affairs because he controls the allocation of water within the village and supervises the maintenance of the local water system. Water is scarce in the summer months and is allocated to households on the basis of family size and additional needs (animals); this predetermined supply flows into each household's cistern once a month. Although there are various control centers on the pipelines throughout the village, these are padlocked and are to be opened only by the president or an employee of the water company.

Disputes over water are particularly common during the summer months and these disputes may originate in several ways. Frequently, individuals will break open the padlocks and allow themselves more water than has been assigned. There are usually strained feelings over the water supply since many families feel that factional grudges and favoritism are involved in the allocation of water. Sometimes individuals break the locks to supplement their water supply and never repair them, whereas others are ordered to make such repairs quickly. Such discretionary action fosters resentment about favoritism toward certain individuals, and frustration over such actions abounds in the village. If the pipelines in a certain area become clogged with sand and debris, families will usually request that the president and the water company employee repair the pipe. Sometimes families must wait several hours or days (if the president is out of town, for example) for repairs. These situations also create hostility and tension. Although repairs to pipelines usually involve a group effort of several men who are willing to help, the authority for such repairs and the ability to turn off the water during repairs rests with the president and the water company. Since all such administrative duties are subject to judgement and discretion, and since the water is always in short supply, there is a constant flow of personal tension and animosity directed toward the influence of the president of the municipality.

A Mediated Case: A Profile

In order to introduce the actual mediation procedures, a detailed case is presented in Case 5. It involves assault with a weapon, serious personal injury, and a Moslem–Christian confrontation. This case illustrates the elaborate procedures and functions of mediation. A detailed discussion of the specific elements of conflict management through mediation will follow.

CASE 5. CROSS-RELIGIOUS ASSAULT WITH A WEAPON

The injured party, Yussef A, is a 57-year-old Christian. The assailant, Ahmad B, is an 18-year-old Moslem.
Yussef and Ahmad were seen arguing in the fields by witnesses. Although the specific issues were not overheard, the quarrel was violent, and Ahmad

A Mediated Case: A Profile

abruptly left the scene. Minutes later a shot was heard. Workers in the field rushed to the scene and found Yussef shot in the leg. Ahmad was seen in a nearby field walking the opposite direction and carrying a machine gun.

Yussef was taken by car to a nearby government hospital by relatives. Male elders from Ahmad's family (Family B) went the same day to the hospital, and later conferred personally with elder males form Yussef's family in Shehaam (Family A). The preliminary discussion focused on the need to settle the case within the village, between the families, and that Ahmad's family would take the necessary steps toward peace and restored relations.

Yussef's family, Family A, agreed to this arrangement and stated that all discussions would be resumed after Yussef was released from the hospital and could take an active part. They advised Ahmad's relatives to keep Ahmad safely hidden until Yussef was released from the hospital, for there were several young men in Yussef's family who would seek revenge if they could locate him.

The police were not informed of the incident, but learned about it through village gossip. Whey they questioned Yussef in the hospital, he stated that he had wounded himself accidentally, and that Ahmad had talked with him, but had left before the accident occurred. The police did not pursue the case further at that time. They questioned him again nearly a week after the incident, but Yussef did not change his story and the police stopped investigating the shooting, although they did not believe Yussef's version of the incident, nor that of the witnesses.

Elders from Ahmad's family visited Yussef three times in the hospital during his first month of convalescence to express their concern, gauge his feelings toward mediation and compensation, and evaluate for themselves the extent of his injury and disability. Ahmad's family proceeded to have a series of informal evening meetings throughout this month with various female and male elders present in order to decide how much they should be prepared to pay for the compensation, since they felt the wrong fell upon Ahmad in this incident. They also discussed how they could best raise the required amount. Individually, women and men talked with other elders of the village and of neighboring villages, comparing the particulars of this case with cases they had seen in the past. When they finally reached a figure through consensus, one of the men, Ahmad's paternal uncle, approached one of Yussef's paternal cousins during an informal discussion over coffee and cigarettes, and mentioned this negotiated figure to gauge his reaction.

If the reaction is favorable, informants say, the family will begin the process of raising the money. If the reaction is strongly negative, a whole new set of discussions must take place informally and in groups in an attempt to reach a new figure or develop new arguments and strategies.

Respected elders from other villages are helpful in this regard for they are able to discuss and advise as relatively neutral third parties, talk freely with both sides in the dispute, and negotiate a reasonable and equitable payment. Although outside villagers are members of regional political coalitions and tied personally to individuals in Shehaam through external networks of alliance, their participation in village mediation is relatively neutral. They desire that peace be reestablished in Shehaam so that their ties in the village remain stable and secure.

On the day of Yussef's release from the hospital, 6 weeks after the shooting incident, one of Ahmad's paternal uncles again talked with various relatives from Family A to determine how long they should wait before formally approaching the family. He was informed that Yussef was well, but tired, and that they should allow a few days to pass before beginning discussions. He was assured, however, that his conciliatory gesture would be conveyed to Yussef's household.

After 10 days had passed, Ahmad's father and various male and female-linked relatives made an informal visit to one of Yussef's cousins. During the course of this visit, Ahmad's father (Abdallah) asked if the next evening would be a good time for their families to meet in order to mediate and settle the violence between them. Because Yussef and his cousins and brothers had agreed that the payment that Family B offered was appropriate, a date was set for the following evening after sunset. The word spread quickly throughout Shehaam and in the neighboring villages.

Following the next evening meal the men of Family A began to gather in Yussef's house. The Christian mayor, a member of Yussef's family through marriage, was present. Men from nearby villages had been involved with the discussions and arrangements as they proceeded; this incident was considered a serious matter of willful assault in which Christian and Moslem relations were involved. These male elders, plus men from neighboring villages who had relations with both Family A and Family B, also began to appear at the appointed time. Altogether there were 21 men from Family A assembled in the formal salon of Yussef's home, plus 7 men from the neighboring villages. Around 8 o'clock, men from Family B arrived together, along with the Moslem mayor and 5 other elders from various Moslem families in Shehaam; together they numbered 23. Ahmad's family and their supporters were seated together in the same area of the room. When they were settled and cigarettes had been passed, discussion began.

The spokesman from Family B, Ahmad's paternal uncle, opened the discussion with statements of regret over the incident, for the pain and inconvenience that Yussef had endured, for the limp that would be with him for the rest of his life, and for the hardship to all members of Yussef's family during his hospitalization and recuperation.

Ahmad sat next to his uncle during these statements. He said nothing directly to any member of Yussef's family, although he sometimes spoke in a low voice to his father who was seated on his other side.

Then men from Ahmad's family and some other Moslem elders began to talk about the history of the two families in Shehaam. They recalled how their various relatives had been good friends during the early war (World War I) and how Abdallah's brother had once saved the life of one of Yussef's nephews. They recalled that although their families occasionally had disagreements or unfortunate incidents between them, such as this recent injury, no argument had ever been so great that it had not been solved, if it had been in the hearts of the families to bring peace from within themselves.

Then followed a brief outline of the background of the assault. Both families spoke, saying that they knew the guilt lay primarily with the young Ahmad because they had carefully checked his account with Yussef and the other witnesses.

Ahmad's paternal uncle explained at some length the motivations of the younger man, arguing that the fault for the incident did not lie entirely with Ahmad. The history of relations between the two families was partially responsible for this violent outburst. This history included the pressure from Yussef and his brothers on Ahmad's father, Abdallah, to collect on an outstanding debt. Ahmad had felt that this pressure was an insult to his father's honor and integrity, linked to a factional opposition between Yussef and his father that originated after Abdallah had borrowed the money from Yussef. All the supporters of Family B agreed that such feelings of shame and resentment were no justification for the youth to assault Yussef when he argued with him in the fields.

In addition, Ahmad's youth and impulsiveness were cited by his family as considerations. Many different elders from Family B made statements during this discussion, some men making new points or strengthening the statements of others, some merely reiterating previous statements. Any one of the elders and members of Family A were entitled to make statements if they wished, and many of the statements concerning family history and relations were strongly supported and elaborated by various individuals in the assembled group.

In conclusion, Ahmad's uncle summarized in a statement:

"We realize that you are esteemed and reasonable men in this place (Yussef and his family) and because you, too, realize that these reasons we have talked about are true, you in your honorable way have chosen not to make this anger public and have our son arrested and humiliated. And for this act of nobility in your time of pain and difficulty, we are truly grateful and receptive.

"God willing, your leg will pain you less as time goes on, and God willing, you will again honor us with your evenings.

"And because we know that you believe it is true and valued what we say, that argument is the cleanser of hearts, we know you will accept our apologies, sorrows, and good will and let this matter be finished between us."

During these concluding remarks, in which a proverb was used to complete the argument in a verbal and traditional way, a leather pouch was passed from Abdallah, through the hands of his brother, uncle, and two cousins, into the hands of the visiting elders, and finally into the hands of Yussef himself. Yussef did not open the pouch, but placed it under his cushion and continued to listen. By this simple act he acknowledged and accepted the payment in compensation for his injury (6000 LL/$2000).

When Ahmad's family finished their remarks, Yussef himself made a brief statement, partially reiterating the statement that had preceded.

"I was shocked, of course, as you all would be, that such a thing would happen between Ahmad and me, for I have known him since the day he was born, and in fact, my wife and sister helped his mother in his birth.

"But anger is a powerful force and we have all been angry. And even though I will always walk with this stick, the deed has been done—God help us all. There is no reason or usefulness in my thinking, and may God be merciful and compassionate, to continue the bad blood between us.

"Our families have always met our obligations, have kept our word, debt, and honor, and have given our word and support to one another. God is my witness.

"And so I, and my sons, and my brothers, and my cousins—and all our family accept your gift and your apology. Let us talk no more of this incident."

At this point in the proceedings, Ahmad rose from the floor and was accompanied by his father to the place where Yussef was sitting. He sat on the floor facing Yussef; his father sat at his side. A basin of hot water was brought in by one of the men who had been sitting near the door, along with lather, a straight razor, a shaving brush, and a towel. Yussef then proceeded to make lather and shave the younger man with the straight razor in the presence of the assembled group. Ahmad had removed his outer robe to be lathered and shaved, and a new, white one was brought from another room in Yussef's house. When the ritual shaving was completed, Ahmad dressed in the new white robe; it was his to keep. When all was completed, Ahmad and his father returned and sat among their kinsmen and supporters.

The atmosphere was now less formal and almost relaxed. Men began talking about crops, weather, politics, and farm equipment while they waited for coffee to be served. Cigarettes and loose tobacco were again passed around, although most men carry their own. Soon coffee was brought in and served by one of the younger daughters of Yussef's household. In this particular case it was more than 3 hours, or well past 10 o'clock, when the coffee was finished. Because the following day was a working day, the men began to leave after a short period of time. They found their shoes and sandals on the porch, said goodnight to one another, shook Yussef's hand and left the house, leaving only a few relatives to talk later into the night about their impressions of the night's events.

These relatives thought that the higher moral values of the community had been reiterated and restored, and the families had been relieved of the burden of overt conflict and dissension, at least over this particular issue. The shaving ceremony, which is no longer used routinely in Shehaam, gave symbolic expression to the acceptance by the injured party (Yussef) of the apologies and compensation. When he performed this menial service, and when the opposing party placed his life literally in his hands under the razor, the injured person signified that the two men were again equal with no animosity between them. In this way, they said, relationships are continually restored through mediation without dealing summarily with all the tensions of the village and community, although the underlying causes of conflict still remain. In this case, the tension and disagreement between Yussef and Abdallah over the unpaid debt still remains unresolved. It would be impossible, Yussef and his relatives stated that night, to alleviate all the tensions and hostilities in the village. Villagers feel that mediation is a more practical, workable solution for procuring fast, efficient, equitable, and cheap resolution to devisive and potentially destructive incidents.

Most elements of the management of conflict contained in this case are common ones. These are the disregard for the amount of elapsed time, the oscillating movements of mediators between one party and the other, the knowledge of family history and underlying motives, the equalizing of family status through reiteration of family histories, the willingness of both parties to settle through mediation, and the willingness to listen to the entire dispute from both parties for as long as it takes to satisfy everyone. These qualities characterize mediation in Shehaam, whether it lasts two hours or goes on for months. The shaving ritual and gift of a white garment are much less frequent occurrences in recent years, although they used to be regular parts of any prolonged mediation involving serious injury or death. Such traditional practices are now considered old fashioned by many villagers, although they may be included if either party, but especially the injured party, requests them.

Procedures

The range of supporters involved in a dispute depends on relationships within the family, the structure of the litigants' personal support networks, and the type of dispute. Acts of physical violence—assault, homicide, hit and run—are defined as serious offenses because "blood has been spilled" and the overall integrity of the community has been shaken.

When such a serious incident occurs, male relatives of the disputing parties meet spontaneously, in twos or in groups, as soon as news of the incident spreads. Not all male relatives necessarily convene. It is at this initial stage that factional splits within families, support networks, and the type of dispute begins to filter individual supporters and mediators.

In a family dispute, only close relatives gather to discuss it. Other extended family members may be asked to join, but this is at the discretion of the parties. In family disputes, except in the rare case of homicide, only elder male relatives and males closely related through marriage have the duty to gather formally in the defense of the family. This insular nature of families is routinely observed and members of other families will not enter into negotiations unless specifically consulted.

In disputes between husbands and wives, women look to other women in their household and work group for support. If this does not eventually yield results, the woman will consult with her mother, aunts, and then uncles if they are residents of the village. The pattern for men is the same; they consult with close male relatives and friends. A woman's relatives will visit her husband and his close relatives in order to try to effect a negotiated compromise if the marital disputing continues or escalates to violence. If this informal process is unsatisfactory, a woman may leave the household and return to her family, whether or not they are located in the village. Her husband must then formally negotiate with her family and often offer his wife satisfactory gifts before she will agree to return.

If she does not agree to return, she may stay in her parents' house with their permission, or she may go to live with a sibling, ususally a married sister. This depends on the discretion of the parents. There have been cases when a woman's father refuses her permanent shelter if she is married and/or has several small children to care for.

Men may leave the household, also, and they generally return to their father's house where they are accepted indefinitely until the domestic argument is resolved or divorce is initiated. In such cases all immediate family members are involved in the proceedings; members of a personal network may be consulted on a personal basis, but this discussion and support is sought informally, and is separate from joint family deliberations.

If the dispute is between members of two different families, then close relatives, in an individual's support network, and non-kin members of the network will gather randomly in small groups to discuss the dispute and formulate strategies. These gatherings usually end up sexually segregated if more then 10 people are present, with the women and men engaging in separate coffee and conversation; this is the preference on both sides, although men and women do discuss these issues at meetings together among the family at informal times such as meals, coffee, or evening relaxation.

As people begin gathering, the extent of the violence and injury are the first facts to be clearly determined in any dispute. It is critical that the two primary actors in the dispute do not meet at this time in order to avoid further violence. If one or more parties have been hospitalized, informal caucusing continues after it is verified that the injured party wishes a mediated settlement, but formal proceedings must wait until the injured party returns home.

If no one is hospitalized, the male elders first to to the home of the victim and listen to an account of the incident. If the real victim is not obvious, they proceed first to the house of the oldest party. They then move to the home of the other disputant and follow the same procedure of listening and asking pointed questions when accounts are unclear or contradictory. They continue the discussion and fact-finding back and forth in this manner until the facts of the case begin to emerge in a clear fashion, and they are assured that the conflict will lie dormant until an agreement can be reached peacefully between the two parties, their families, and the group of mediators.

While the men engage in these activities, the women gather in another area—knitting, drinking coffee— and discuss the dispute as well as other current topics of interest. They share facts and speculations that they have heard from neighbors, in overheard family conversations, and in discussions with various family members. This information is often discussed among the women of each household as they prepare dinner, and again as a topic during the family dinner. In this way, discussion at this fact-finding stage progresses through a series of large and small, sexually segregated and mixed groups of people sharing information and opinions.

In cases of general community concern such as homicide, injury, protracted violence and feuds, male elders from the village and surrounding region converge in the appropriate village to participate in the procedure.

After the spontaneous discussions following the outbreak of a dispute, the next step is to collect and weigh the evidence, then review the history of the disputants and their families. These discussions proceed along the same lines of individual and joint discussion. Then, during lengthy discussions lasting days, weeks, or even months, the mediators and discussants weight the merits of the particular case. It is important that all persons discussing the case have some knowledge of a large range of disputes that have occurred in the area, for it is from this body of precedents that criteria of intent, negligence, reasonable behavior, and payment standards are drawn. Women and men participate in these extensive debates leading to resolution, as this period of the process continues to occur at random times throughout the days that follow, either in the households over coffee, in public gathering places (shops, or the local oven), or in the fields.

The agreement is reached gradually through shared information and consensus (see Bailey, 1965). If accounts of the dispute from the parties and witnesses vary in substance, it is the duty of the women and men closest to the disputing individuals through kinship or support networks to help uncover the truth of the matter. This is accomplished either through informal examination of witnesses or direct investigation.

Witnesses may be found and checked for their accuracy. The disputing parties are also questioned repeatedly, usually by their immediate family, but kin with influence can participate and they usually do not wait to be asked. In this way discrepancies and contradictions appear over time and are narrowed down by the families. This procedure is often lengthy, allowing tempers to cool among the disputing parties, informants say, so that a reasonable outcome can be accepted and appreciated by everyone concerned. Such extended use of time has been discussed in various geographic locations in the broader context of decision making and the process of reaching compromise and consensus opinions (Starr, 1970, 1978a, 1978b; Yngvesson, 1970).

If a dispute comes to the attention of the local police, their reports require statements from a minimum of two witnesses. Records indicate that witnesses are uninformative and uncooperative in police investigations. During mediation conducted by villagers, as in the informal personal investigations made by the mayor, witnesses make detailed accounts that often take hours to verify. In a dispute or assault occurring in a highly populated area, varying accounts are often too voluminous to handle. In such cases, reliable sources are sought who are respected, even-tempered, and, preferably, have no direct relation to the disputing parties.

Investigations

In cases when the second party or respondent is initially unknown, as in the two cases of theft discussed in relation to the mayor's duties, informal investigation and fact-finding is initiated. This fact-finding process does not always run smoothly, and witnesses are not always eager to assist village investigations. Cooperation depends on the type of dispute; people are less likely to want to involve themselves in domestic, insult, or slander cases, for example. Cooperation also depends on the degree to which networks and alliances are threatened. Generally, the less an individual or family is pressured politically, the more willing they are to assist in investigation. Although false testimony is sometimes given during a local investigation, it does not have tremendous and long-range impact because of the volume and depth of questioning that occurs within the village. All statements are cross-checked and conflicting or malevolent motives are confronted.

Women play an integral part in investigations taking place in the village. The diversity of women's daily work takes them over a vaster range of territory around the village. Women frequently go to the ovens, the butchers, the shops, and in and out of the village to work in the vineyards. Therefore, women see a greater variety of activities in the village than the men who are at home or at work in the fields. Women can usually accurately recall the movements of individuals at various times of day, particularly if those movements seemed suspicious at the time. Many cases of petty theft are solved when the investigators find the woman who was working in the area of the theft on that particular day. Very often a woman has actually witnessed the theft, but has kept silent waiting for the theft to be discovered and made public.

In cases of serious theft, and/or when the local mayor is not immediately available, such as in the theft of sheep, the injured family may organize itself to investigate the evidence. Tracks of the animals are followed, if possible, and remains of the carcass are sought in the surrounding mountain area. Sheep are frequently stolen as a prank or as an overt act of hostility brought on by factional competitions between families. While there are poor families in Shehaam who rarely eat meat, they rely on more fortunate relatives to supply these needs. Animal thieves do not steal to survive; they steal to irritate.

Sometimes the thieves are caught red-handed eating the meat or trying to bury the feet, tail, and head after the meat has been sold or transported. Sometimes, too, blood can be found on the thieves' clothing, as the previous case illustrated, if investigations are begun soon after the incident.

Whatever the form of investigation, thieves are confronted with evidence when it is convincing. In order to make a personal confrontation, men from the injured family will consult with other men from their own family, from related families, and frequently from neutral nonfamily elders. This is done so that the respondent is not confronted only by hostile and accusing family members. Inclusion of extra people also minimizes the fabrication of evidence against an individual, and early thorough investigation makes it hard for a thief to later destroy evidence of a theft.

As the previous case of stolen sheep illustrated, when a family is confronted with an accusation, the act and the type of investigation that has been conducted is explained and the respondent's family is told that compensation is expected. Once the confrontation has been made public in this manner, the same general discussion and consensus procedure is followed.

A just compensation is agreed upon by the accused party's family if they judge him or her to be responsible for the infraction, and eventually a sum of money is paid. The incident will be briefly reviewed by both families in discussion and the money in compensation will be handed directly to the complainant when these discussions are completed to everyone's satisfaction. Coffee will be served and drunk together as a symbolic gesture of friendship and good will, and the matter will be considered closed.

If the evidence is circumstantial and the wrong person(s) accused, this will become clear as the family confrontations and consensus discussions proceed. If this is the case, a new investigation is initiated, usually with the falsely accused party and family actively participating.

Sanctions

Homicide and assault involving injury are the kinds of cases when the "blood relations between families is most strained." In cases involving a large amount of money as payment in compensation (usually over $200), the evidence and deliberations must be clear and the motives, norms, and behavior clearly understood by all participants. The stage is then properly set for the mending of social relations. Mediation is particularly important in these cases in restoring internal order and reaffirming group norms.

The minimum amount for any human life, woman, man, or child, taken either accidentally or by willful act, is approximately $2000. This basic figure is increased by increments as various circumstances surrounding the death or injury are clarified. A rough index of such circumstances and their relative monetary sanctions compiled from observed and elicited case material is given in Table 4.1.

Although the circumstances are arranged in order of increasing seriousness as villagers define them, the monetary range is more flexible. The figures are not fixed, but represent the financial ranges of the recorded cases in the sample.

The mediators, after determining the facts and listening to both sides, ask the bereaved family the amount they believe is reasonable to compensate them for their family's loss. A family could not ask $50,000 in payment for a death; it would not be judged reasonable. Based on past cases, the mediators would ask, "Why are you asking $50,000? Is your mother or brother better than ours?" As the index in Table 4.1 indicates, the price varies according to circumstances, but is not allowed to rise to an impossible figure. For example, if the price asked is

TABLE 4.1
Relevant Circumstances in Determining Compensation in Cases of Death or Injury

Circumstances	Approximate payment scale in U.S. dollars[a]
Death, accidental	1500
Death, accidental, negligence	1800–2000
Homicide, in argument	2000
Homicide, premeditated (victim aware of on-going dispute)	2200–2500
Homicide, premeditated or ambush (victim unaware of on-going dispute)	2700
Injury, accidental	75–150 + medical fees
Injury, willful, 1 month recovery	175 + medical fees
Injury, willful, 2 months recovery	350–850
Injury, willful, 6 months recovery	850–1500
Injury, willful, extensive recovery and/or disability	1750 and up

[a] 1 U.S. dollar = 3 Lebanese pounds (L.L.).

$2000, this price is unnegotiable as long as it is judged reasonable. Reasonableness is determined by the consensus of the mediators. After a just figure is agreed on, it is conveyed to the guilty party and his or her family by the mediators. If they cannot meet this price, there are two alternative solutions.

First, the mediators and several male elders from the accused family will go to the bereaved family and explain their economic circumstances. They would indicate that they wished to honorably settle the matter, but were unable to pay the requested amount. The mediators would then talk with the injured family to lower the price to a more workable figure, say $1000 to $1500, instead of the original $2000. One argument they are likely to use is:

> "Your family is well-respected and known for their justice, honor, and nobility in these matters. Here is a poor man who cannot reasonably pay the amount you ask.
> "We ask you, as a honorable man, as your neighbors and relatives, for our sakes and for the sake of peace and harmony among our families and in our land, that you consent to take a lower figure, say $1000, which to this family is like $4000."

An honorable family may eventually yield to these requests with some compromise, saying something equivalent to:

> "Praise be to God, for your sakes, those of you who have gathered here for so long to settle this affair, I will accept $1500 and the affair will be finished."

After all this discussion, however, if the injured party's family will still not agree to lower the price, either because of stubborness, honor, or strong emotional commitment to the dead or seriously injured family member, the money will be raised among the mediators who have gathered to settle the dispute. That is, they will pay the difference between the agreed price and what the accused's family can reasonably pay. Such collective payment does not make the accused's family obligated to the mediators and their families in an economic or political sense, although this is one of the unstated bonds of reciprocity that binds families from the community into the mediation process. Responsibility for such payment also gains the mediators respect and honor within the entire village.

Furthermore, this method is effective in preventing a family from holding out for a lower payment if they can reasonably pay the required amount. To say that "we will pay your debt for you because you are honestly poor and truly cannot pay" will cause shame and dishonor in a family that is holding out against paying an amount they can afford. If this should be the case, the family, out of shame and pressure from relatives, will usually capitulate and pay the full amount on the day of mediation or reimburse the mediators individually at a later date to save face and prove themselves honorable.

Case Material

Table 4.2 presents cases from a 10-year period (1963–1973). The cases were either observed (17) or elicited from the memory of informants (197). The only changes made in village classification or disputes were to separate multiple categories: If a case involved slander and property damage, it appears in Table 4.2 as two separate entries. Both parties in all these disputes are residents of the village.

None of these cases were reported to the local police, although some were discovered by the police on their own initiative (21 of 196). For these discovered cases the police made formal written reports, and in some cases initiated investigations, but all cases were ultimately resolved through mediation.

Not all these cases required the prolonged mediation process. In the cases of the two forged deeds, mediation was initiated, but dissolved when it became clear that the errors were mistakes in transcription rather than deliberate fraud. Twelve cases (five debt, four stolen animals, three forged checks) were resolved covertly through influence and persuasion, as was illustrated in the two earlier cases involving the mayor, Elias.

Theft and physical assault are by far the most prevalent types of disputes. Insult ranks third, ranking closer in frequency to theft and assault than these figures reveal because many insult cases have not been mediated and are not included in this tabulation. Many insults remain active and are a primary source of interpersonal tension and hostility. The other types of cases with statistical significance are illegal use of water, disputed property boundaries, debts, and illegal use of land. This distribution illustrates how scarce economic resources predominate among the major issues that draw most individuals into open conflict.

Over one-quarter of the disputes are between Christians and Moslems. Every effort is made to resolve such disputes without resorting to police or court authorities. These mediated cases are in direct contrast to the police records in this regard, for the police records list only a small percentage of cross-religious disputes. Christian–Moslem disputes are much less likely to become formal and public as entries on the police record. The application of formal, external authority to cross-religious cases could potentially polarize positions among disputing parties because of the court's tendency to decide in a win or lose manner; this would effectively split the village in half. Villagers have a strong, nearly unanimous preference to mediate such disputes locally because of concern for the internal balance of village relations. Processes such as mediation or investigation on the part of the mayor, which re-integrate village relationships, are an overwhelming preference in these types of potentially volatile cases. The possible used of public disclosure will be discussed in Chapter 5.

Women and the Disputing Process

Women in Shehaam are hard-working, strong, volatile, durable, humorous, and warm. They are quick to anger, as are men, and they engage in conflict with a vitality and tenacity that usually astounds Westerners. Women's lives can be full and rich from their own perspective, but the reader should not romanticize. The frustrations felt in a setting that values endurance, strength, and longevity, but creates conflict for a woman who wishes to compete and advance in the men's world, are both personal and structural. The culture prescribes that women should be both nurturing and hard-working. Women who realize their skills, strengths, and resources as productive individuals often find it frustrating that they compete, challenge, and succeed politically in a sphere separate from the power-dominant male sphere (see Dwyer, 1977, 1979; Mernissi, 1975).

The status and political systems for men and women are, as noted earlier, complimentary and intersecting. Although politically competitive spheres are sexually segregated, direct confrontation between the sexes occurs because the needs and goals of individual men and women are never mutually exclusive.

Outsiders often wonder where Middle Eastern women get the energy to argue, harangue, and fight with such intensity. Based on formal interviews and long talks with many women of different ages, the women's consensus is that arguing is fun, diverting, energizing, and stimulating. These women are very aware of the broader political context and stratification by sex, but engaging in disputes can be very satisfying. Disputes give women personal ventilation for the frustrations of daily life, and also reaffirm their position in the sociopolitcal network that laces the village together. In fact, a good indicator of the seriousness of a dispute is by observing the women's behavior. If the women of disputing households are sharing minimal social interaction, such as drinking coffee or sharing a bread oven, family conflict is superficial and will be resolved as a matter of course through informal discussion and caucusing. If the women have severed relations with each other, the conflict runs deeper, will be protracted, and will require resolution by mediation.

In the case materials collected, women are most often involved in disputes of insult, slander, debt, and animal theft. Most of the disputes involving women as either party occur within the village boundaries rather than in the fields. (Exceptions were three exchanges of insults while harvesting and a physical fight between two women while picking potatoes in the fields.) In the six cases where women were involved in animal theft, these thefts were the result of both per-

TABLE 4.2
Locally Mediated Disputes in Shehaam: 1963-1973

Type of case	Police action (Percentage of total)	Christian (Percentage of total)	Moslem (Percentage of total)	Christian–Moslem (Percentage of total)	Total cases	Total percentage
Theft						
Animals	1	36	36	28	28	14
Property	13	50	50	—	8	4
Crops	—	43	36	21	14	7
Physical assault						
No injury	—	25	25	50	4	2
Injury	30	26	35	39	23	12
Physical assault with weapon	13	27	27	46	15	8
Insult	—	33	39	28	18	9
Illegal use of water	15	38	24	38	13	7
Debt	—	37	45	18	11	6
Property boundaries	18	45	45	10	11	6

68

Illegal use of land	30	40	40	20	10	5
Property damage	—	38	38	24	8	4
Crop damage	—	24	38	38	8	4
Marital disputes						
Argument, insult	—	50	50	—	2	1
Assault	—	50	50	—	2	1
Flight	—	25	75	—	4	2
Slander	—	57	29	14	7	4
Hit and run						
Death	100	—	100	—	1	—
Injury	33	33	66	—	3	2
Forgery						
Checks	33	66	33	—	3	2
Deeds	—	100	—	—	2	—
Homicide	—	—	100	—	1	—
	N = 21	N = 72	N = 74	N = 50	N = 196	N = 100%

Source: Witty, 1978.

sonal political rivalries between individual women, and extensions of rivalries between families as a result of political alliances.

Conflicts that periodically are expressed as verbal insults are indicative of prolonged political rivalries and are not amenable to easy resolutions. Periodic mediation and group discussion is required in these types of cases—to keep situational anger contained—even though the underlying tensions may remain. In the discussions around such protracted conflicts, women and men usually talk in single-sex groups as they work together during the day. Respected women elders are often consulted by younger women in disputes and quarrels of this kind, and previous examples of problem solving within the family have illustrated that men often need and consult such older women as well.

As the mediation process develops, men take the public role in formalized proceedings and women are currently content with men performing this role. Even when women are actively involved as parties and discussants, mediation is formally organized by men of the respective families. This public control by men is to protect the women's interests, say the men, so that women will not be subjected to anger or improper interaction with nonfamily members. All 20 of the women interviewed on this topic were content to let the men publically handle disputes. Women uniformly gave three reasons for this: (*a*) they felt that men could argue strongly in public, whereas some women were hesitant to do so in front of strangers (although they argue vigorously elsewhere), (*b*) men were more knowledgeable and skilled in mediation discussions because they took part in them frequently, and (*c*) mediation gave the men something important to discuss and pursue in their leisure time.

Case 6 is the only case that I observed of physical assaults between two women that was publicly mediated by male elders from both families. It will illustrate that in cases involving women, as in *all* cases involving prolonged family discussion, women play a crucial role in the successful rebuilding of social ties.

CASE 6. A CASE OF INSULT AND VILOLENCE BETWEEN WOMEN

Two young Moslem women, Fatuum (30 years old and divorced) and Saydi (26 years old and unmarried), related through marriage, met on the road from the village to the fields. Fatuum was returning from the fields with a large bag of potatoes and Saydi was going to the fields with food supplies for her father and brothers. Saydi was accompanied by the ethnographer.

Fatuum started the incident by shouting sexual insults at Saydi as they approached each other on the road. Saydi did not take this lightly, but started hitting Fatuum with a large metal pan. A physical struggle followed in which both women were bruised and bloodied around the face and arms before they could be separated. The ethnographer tried to separate the women, and three Christian women following close behind Fatuum

Women and the Disputing Process

came to the assistance of the ethnographer more than to the assistance of one of the fighting women. The fight was finally stopped after much shouting and screaming, and both injured women and the other women who intervened returned to the village.

Saydi's family considered her to be the injured party. Because of Fatuum's unspeakable insults, she and her family had been publicly shamed and dishonored.

Fatuum's male relatives proceeded on the same assumption since Fatuum had been physically struck first. The women returned to their parents' homes and began shouting and crying their accounts of the incident to those present; the women gathered around and cleansed the injuries and the men began planning a strategy after they had heard the firsthand version. The women and men physically separated to different parts of the house as these activities evolved for each.

[Note: The background to this fight reveals that both women were to some degree provoked by past history. Fatuum's ex-husband and Saydi were the subject of rumors throughout the village, and the worst version of these rumors made Saydi responsible for Fatuum's husband's departure and subsequent divorce. Fatuum has four children, ages 9, 8, 6, and 4, and although she receives some support from her husband and his family for the children ($20 a month), her prospects for remarriage seem slim to her and she has a hard time making ends meet financially. She works in the fields for wages and crop payments, but this work is hard and seasonal. During the winter she sells cow milk locally (she has two cows) and depends on her family for additional support.

Saydi's somewhat biased view is that Fatuum is a nag and a gossip, and not worth speaking to; however, she does have hopes of marrying Fatuum's former husband.

The way the resolution of this case progressed is interesting because it illustrates the separate and complimentary spheres of power and influence for women and men.

The men depicted in Figure 4.1 are the men in both families who were centrally involved in formally mediating this dispute. The women depicted worked together and on behalf of the injured woman from their family to overcome each disputant's resistance to a settlement.]

The women, all of whom informally spoke with personal friends as well as the family members shown, ultimately pulled together two arguments that eventually carried weight for each of the disputing women.

The first argument was that the alleged hard feelings and angers under question are a common dilemma for women in general. This was the more personal argument and it basically offered support, understanding, and empathy from the women in the family, along with the implied argument that "no man is worth it."

The second point of persuasion was the fact that some of the women

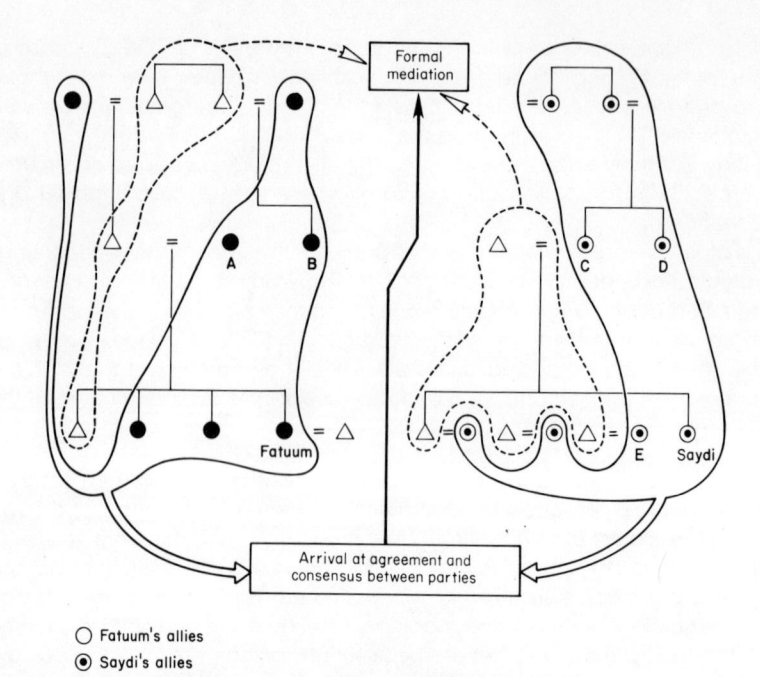

72   4. Conflict Management and Dispute Settlement: The Mediation Process

FIGURE 4.1. Physical assault between two women.

○ Fatuum's allies
● Saydi's allies

from these two families, Persons A, B, C, D, and E, were directly allied in a political network with other women, in periodic opposition to another long-standing faction of women from a different family. The women strongly interested in this alliance did not want it severed because of a simple altercation between two of the younger women in their families. This was a secondary argument, but it was used.

The combination of these two points of view finally achieved a consensus among all the women, after the disputing women had cooled their anger. Discussions with the two women took place with their fathers and brothers present the first day, but cooling the tempers and working toward agreement was accomplished by the women of each respective family. These women kin were warm and supportive to the injured women, and continued to talk with them singly or in small informal groups as they worked and lived together.

Meanwhile, the fathers and brothers of the two women met initially to discuss who had initiated the argument, who was the most seriously injured, and which actions were provoked or motivated by events in family history. These men had one heated, exploratory session, and a second session in which the mayor and three other nonrelated male elders were present. All tentatively agreed at this second meeting that the injuries and various insults were about the same for each woman and family, and that the women should apologize to one another. Both sets of men left agreeing they would meet again if this was possible—each personally knowing that this was much easier said than done. For the men, the process halted at this point for several weeks, while the women cooled off and their lives went on.

After nearly 6 weeks, the women did come together at a formal resolution session. The male kin involved and the mayor were present, and each woman was accompanied by her mother and maternal grandmothers. They apologized briefly to one another, coffee was served, and the immediate incident was put behind them. Fatuum and Saydi are still not friendly, but they now try to avoid one another.

Thus, while it has been noted that informal consenses must be reached before the final mediation/resolution meeting can occur, this incident illustrates how movement from one stage to another is certainly not the sole activity of male mediators and male elders. The direct power and influence of women varies in degrees depending on the people involved and the type of case, but that power is always there. Women have also successfully delayed or blocked mediation proceedings through political maneuvering and they have clear personal and political power to wield a protracted dispute case.

Women's lives in Shehaam are not perfect or easy from their perspective or from ours, but the segregation of sexes in Middle Eastern cultures does generate two dialectical forces. One has already been mentioned—the personal and political frustration of being outside the culturally dominant political group, even though women compete and align successfully with other women. The second force is the closeness and solidarity that exists among women as a group or class of individuals. Women in Sheheam value one another, understand something of the commonality of women's positions in the area, and know that it is often preferable to form strong alliances with other women. This alliance building is true with kin and non-kin.

If women in Sheheam ever seek and achieve public power, they will be an especially strong force to reckon with. Such a movement among Middle-Eastern women would have a pretested solidarity that would not be terribly vulnerable to internal division. Movements in Iran and Egypt in the 1970s indicate that such solidarities are rapidly becoming social and political realities.

Conclusions

To dispel the impression that all disputes become systematized and formalized in the manner just described, I would like to include an example of a case that illustrates the general use of mediational skills in interpersonal relationships

(Case 7). The use of such skills is not limited to adults; children practice mediation and consensus-building in play and in actual resolution of playtime squabbles.

CASE 7. THE CASE OF THE MISUNDERSTOOD DEBT

Najib's family had just finished dinner and he sent his youngest son, Sam, to fetch 30 LL from Hassan M., which was still owed for some stone work Najib had finished the week before. Najib wanted the money for food supplies for the Ramadan feasting that was approaching.

About 5 minutes later, Hassan M. appeared in the doorway, asking what 30 LL he owes. He thought he had paid Najib in full (50 LL) already.

There followed a long and heated discussion what they had originally agreed. Najib insisted the work is paid "by the meter," and Hassan M. had calculated on a daily basis. Najib told him to ask anybody who has built anything lately to quote him a price, and he would be glad to abide by that. Then Hassan M. countered with the argument that he knew people who had paid less for similar work, although it was a few years ago.

Then Najib reached deep into his pocket and threw back the 50 LL note he had originally been paid. Hassan M. threw it back, and the bill changed hands twice again before Najib changed tactics; he began a calm, itemized listing of what work he had done, the supplies he had bought, and the building process.

At this point, two neighbors arrived at the door, Salim and Butros. They entered and were greeted. They sat down and lit cigarettes and then asked if there was anything wrong. Najib and Hassan M. repeated their arguments. Hassan M. kept repeating that the price Najib was quoting was too much, but he did not say how much he expected to pay, or what he thought the job was worth.

After both parties had completed the full extent of their comments, Salim and Butros asked a few questions of each. During the questioning they said that they felt Najib had done the work for almost nothing, 20 LL over the cost of the supplies that he purchased and brought to the site as a favor to Hassan M. Salim then pointed out that the cost of wood had risen considerably, and that what Najib was asking for supplies and labor was cheap; he added further that he could not believe that Hassan M. was complaining about anything.

Then both parties went through their versions of the situation again, quietly, although Hassan M. was losing some steam in the second retelling of his position.

Finally, Salim and Butros had to agree that Najib had been more than fair, and that Hassan M. should pay him the additional 30 LL and end the matter. They pointed out how much similar work had cost them and others around them, and they spent a great deal of time discussing the current cost of building materials (there was a 20-minute discussion of this point alone).

Conclusions

Hassan M. was still shouting occasionally, but it was clear that he had lost his case. The discussion went on, however, with Salim and Butros continuing to ask Najib questions, while Hassan M. sat in silence.

The tea which had been brought in by Najib's wife early in the discussion and was now cold was served, and everyone except Hassan M. drank during the calmer and more reasoned discussion that continued.

Finally Butros asked Hassan M. if he was going to pay the additional 30 LL and settle this very simple matter. Hassan M. said yes he would, but he did not have it right now and would pay Najib in 2 or 3 days. Then both Salim and Butros urged him to drink his tea, as the cup was still untouched. Not to drink it, they told him, would be shameful. The discussion then continued on to other topics; then about 5 minutes later Hassan M. drank the tea down in three large gulps and put his glass back on the tray with the other empty glasses.

That was psychologically the end of the dispute, and although they all stayed about 10 more minutes, the discussion thereafter was more relaxed and friendly. Salim and Butros finally got up to leave, Hassan M. took this opportunity to make his exit as well. Najib, his wife, and mother sat together in the sitting room discussing the situation. Hassan M. had obviously been wrong as far as they were concerned, but they were not so angry as they were frustrated at trying to reason with him. Najib said that he felt like he had been talking to a broken record; Hassan could not think of anything new to say, so he had kept repeating the same points over and over.

In total, the evening's conversation had taken a little over 2 hours. The family was pleased, but exhausted, and decided to go to bed and think no more about the incident.

The containment value of mediation is strong whether the process is short or prolonged, and every elder in the village and regional community feels it is a duty to respond to conflict and violence in a conciliatory role. When elders gather at the home of an injured party and proceed back and forth, and as informal discussion groups proliferate, it is publicly clear that a remedy is in progress. Furthermore, during these preliminary discussions the two disputing parties are kept apart and this separation lessens the possibility of open violence and helps keep village cases mediated and out of public jurisdiction. If a case should become publicly violent, the chances of the police hearing of the incident and initiating an investigation, arresting, and imprisoning the wrongdoers are greatly increased. Although there is a shared willingness among families to resolve disputes through mediation, anger and violence are two emotional components of disputes that villagers appreciate in a realistic and preventative way.

In the space of time required for mediation to be successfully completed, the family physically protects the accused individual from retaliation. Such behavior reaffirms the traditional ideal that one's social rights and political status reside in the power and unity of the family unit. In this way, the authority of the family is strengthened. Although we have seen that some families are internally divided into opposing factions, the family remains an integral part of the individual's alternative means of manipulating her or his social and political environment. By providing protection and shelter during times of crisis, the family binds its members continually to the power and authority structures that are its ideological base. Factions and support networks contain some non-kin alliances and also provide support to individuals in times of crisis and reassessment, but since non-kin members of a support network tend to be temporary, the family ties still provide more permanence and predictability.

This supportive function of mediation can be extended to the community, for the notion of village unity maintained against outsiders is reaffirmed and strengthened through the mediation process, and enables an individual to identify with a sociopolitical unit that is larger than the individual, family, or faction.

Many villagers see local mediation as preferable to police or court action, not only because it is quick and less expensive, but also because many informants find mediation a protective and personally comforting process. The fact that village leadership, elders, elites, and mayors take a continued, personal interest in conciliatory settlements not only reinforces their own sense of status quo, but gives individual's a means of raising or reaffirming their personal importance and self-esteem within the community. When elders plead for consideration and mediation from an individual, and provide understanding and empathy as well, an individual feels good about his or her own social worth in this uncertain, competitive, and changing setting. Such strengthening of one's self-respect and prestige can act to draw an individual closer to the family group, or ironically, it can give a person the impetus she or he needs to break from the family and pursue individual interests.

Villagers also feel that it is an effective means of controlling one's political rivals because it is integral to the community. If rivals are perceived to be getting out of hand—gaining some kind of real or imaginary leverage, or becoming in some way overbearing—there are several strategies to be considered by every villager. A person can create a minor dispute, escalate a preexisting dispute to violence, or force a public confrontation through gossip, insult, or public disclosure (going to the police or the court). These active strategies will generate immediate attention from relatives, political allies, and neutral third parties in order to calm the inflammatory situation. A mediated resolution serves to keep one's opponents off-guard and, temporarily at least, binds them to the revised status quo derived from mediation.

In this sense, creating an open conflict can generate distinct political advantage. Contrary to the manifest function of settling disputes, mediation can also be effectively used to undermine opponents' strategies or to stabilize or realign one's political position. Mediation, then, operates on two levels of social control—first on an interpersonal level to minimize violence and anger by mediating disputes, and second, on a community level to minimize personal and factional competition by providing a mechanism for easing tensions and imbalances within the local political arena.

Thus, mediation is a very reintegrative process in terms of family and community solidarity. In remeshing the social fabric that is continually torn by the devisive behavior of factions and competition over scarce resources, mediation reaffirms an individual's sense of community at various levels of social organization and, at the same time, ameliorates overt grievances and disputes.

Competition over scarce tangible resources tends to be personalized, and disputes over property, stolen animals, and water are frequently the underlying causes of disputes initiated by threats, insults, and slander. This tendency seems to be changing, and in accordance with the theory of mediation, disputes over tangible resources such as money or real property are more likely to proceed to the public arena of police hearing and court proceedings. Mediation is always initiated in these cases, but breaks down in the preliminary discussions. One party, usually the complainant, refuses to compromise over the amount in question, despite the pleadings and pressures already described. While these cases mark the area where mediation breaks down most often, resorting to public disclosure through the police or courts is often used as a threat by the complainant. As we will see in Chapter 5, many of these formal, public disputes over tangible scarce resources are ultimately resolved in a second round of mediation, after confrontation has been initiated in the courts.

Feuding is infrequent in this part of Beqaa Valley, at least in a violent sense. Violent protracted feuding has never occurred in Shehaam, according to informants. Cross-religious disputes could potentially divide the village permanently, as threatened to happen in 1952, and villagers work hard to contain and prevent such situations from arising. Mediation and the gathering of village leadership during Christian–Moslem disputes is much more urgent and efficient for this reason.

There are protracted, unresolved arguments within families in the village, in both the Christian and Moslem communities. These generally have to do with bad feelings, insults, and questions of honor and shame generated by village and regional elections. People have remained stubborn about resolving some of these issues, and the result is that some families do not speak to one another. This enforced silence and symbolic ostracism is maintained, even though the families involved attend village ceremonies with the rest of the village population. Informants say that the only circumstances they can recall where such silent feuds have been broken are an accident where one member of a feuding family helps another, or children or grandchildren who strongly wish to marry.

Thus, we see that mediation and the investigation, sanctioning, caucusing, and maneuvering that accompany it in this setting clearly conform to the theory of mediation. There is an obvious presence of social interaction and shared community understanding, a commonly shared tradition of settling in a private forum, a willingness to explore one's personal wants and needs, a willingness to continue a relationship with the disputing party, and a clear belief in the relative egalitarian nature of personal relationships.

The frequency of interaction within the village grows out of the population stability in the area, as do the shared community values, norms, and understandings that come from being an indigenous member of a community. The stability and organization of the family gives people the safety and identity to explore personal wants and needs. The sense of community, family organization, and population stability also generates a need to continue personal relationships because village life is on-going and relatively self-contained, but the insular, protective nature of these characteristics also reinforces the need to keep strangers and strange values outside, and to settle disputes in a private, nonpublic forum. The personal self-esteem that is reaffirmed for disputing parties during mediation generates an egalitarian perspective, as does the fact that the mediation process operates in identical fashion for all villagers, whether they are rich, poor, landless, large landowners, or members of the elite, elder leadership organization of the village.

We have seen that the pursuit of scarce resources remains tied to local, shared values, but as westernization increases, competition over tangible wealth is the most problematic circumstance for successful mediation. These social and economic changes will be further explored in Chapter 6. The village leadership structures are relatively undifferentiated; leadership is clearly not solely a question of class, wealth, or land ownership. There is a shared expectation that all integral conflict will be resolved internally, and this requires organization and specialization. Organization and specialization assure procedural continuity over time, but the continual addition of diverse numbers of mediators also allows flexibility and change in a long-term perspective. The political implication of general social change and specific economic changes in the region will be discussed in Chapter 6 as well.

The failure or partial failure of mediation allows disputes to emerge from the protective community, and become a matter of police and court records. It is that aspect of the theory of mediation, when it will not work successfully, that we turn our attention to in Chapter 5.

5
The Police and the Courts

Although the people of Shehaam have a highly developed mediation process for the local management of conflict, they live in a rapidly changing social environment. Constant contact with the world outside the village is provided through television, radio, and newspapers. Personal support networks extend outside the village, linking individuals to political figures, bureaucrats, family members, and other allies. The formal legal system, the courts, lawyers, and police are part of this expanded world of relations that villagers must deal with daily.

Courts and lawyers are relevant to villagers' lives as alternatives *within* village-centered mediation. Villagers are increasingly becoming involved, voluntarily and involuntarily, with the conflict and power of the larger political world. Powerful business and government interests use their power, knowledge, and the law to develop their own interests in neighborhoods, suburbs, and villages. The ability or lack of ability to deal with these consolidated power interests is critical to how villages like Shehaam grow and change. Internal conflict can be handled equitably at the village and community levels or matter how complex the case or how strained the relations between the parties. As we have seen, however, mediation requires, among other things, a shared set of values and a willingness to resolve the conflict through internal conciliatory means. Government and business do not generally share the belief that these two prerequisites are necessary in settling breaches of statutes and regulations through mediation. Villagers will not be able to continue incorporating the courts into local mediation-proceeding mechanisms indefinitely without loss of political force in the larger system. Contact with the police is the most frequent way of entering into the formal legal process, and understanding the police role in the community brings the relationship between villagers and the formal legal system into sharper focus. In certain types of cases involving tangible scarce resources, mediation is less successful as a local remedy agent. Conditions under which mediation is less effective than adjudication will be explored as well.

The Police

The police station in Shehaam is physically located in the Catholic community in an old building rented from, and adjacent to, the Catholic church. None of the eight police officers or the police chief are residents of Shehaam. Police officials are purposely chosen from outside local jurisdictions in order to insure neutrality and minimize bias in the enforcement of the law.

The police made daily rounds in Shehaam, the surrounding villages, and the fields. These routine patrols are organized to keep policemen aware of tensions and disputes within the area, to look for visible property or crop damage that may lead to a dispute, and to allow individuals to talk with the police and possibly report actions for police investigation. In practice, the police visit with local shopkeepers in the surrounding villages and in Shehaam, drink coffee in a nearby coffeehouse, and generally make their presence felt. They attempt through casual questioning to discover if any violence has occurred since their last patrol, or if there are any impending fights that should be controlled.

Most people are reluctant to reveal information about disputes to the police. This reluctance is based not so much on apprehension as it is on the principle that outside agents should not be concerned or involved with local disputes between inhabitants of the community. A large portion of the police's time, therefore, is spent on patrol trying to find out what is going on in the community. The police station in Shehaam always has an officer on duty so that formal complaints can be reported at any time.

There are two ways a dispute becomes a case in the written police records. Either the police witness and record a disturbance on their daily patrols, or individuals come to the station and file a formal complaint. Two witnesses are required for all such complaints, but because their testimony is usually so vague and noncommittal, the recording of such testimony is, in most cases, a mere formality.

The police cases compiled from Shehaam cover a 9-year period from 1965 through 1973 (Table 5.1) and were taken from the written police records. A number of features from these records are striking.

Of the total 160 cases recorded in the last 9 years involving parties from Shehaam, only 28 cases involved village members as both parties. That is, only

TABLE 5.1
Police Cases: Distribution of Participants[a]

	Reaching outside village boundary		Contained within village boundary	
	Percentage of total	Number of cases	Percentage of total	Number of cases
Between persons	36	59	18	28
State versus individual	46	73	—	—
		132 cases		28 cases

Source: Witty, 1978.
[a] $N = 160$.

18% of the police cases over this 9-year period were the result of individuals from Shehaam filing formal complaints against other villagers.

Cases initiated by the state against individuals on civil matters (46%) constituted nearly half the "outside" complaint category; villagers' disputes with nonresidents comprised the other half.

Such state-initiated cases predominantly involve administrative control. These administrative violations specifically include building without a permit, illegal sale of tobacco (selling directly without paying sales tax), illegal possession of weapons, illegal opening of water pipes, blockage of a public road, disturbing the peace, and operating a business without a permit. Lebanese authorities consider such cases civil because they do not involve actions against other people. Fines rather than imprisonment are the common type of sanction applied to these cases. Many civil permit matters are public formal police complaints because villagers refuse to heed warnings from the police that such a complaint will be filed if he or she does not comply with building codes. Such behavior is not mere stubbornness on the part of the villagers, but a realistic understanding that the fine for a building violation is much smaller than the cost of the permit. Once the fine is paid, the state drops the complaint, so by allowing the complaint to proceed to an arrest, villagers calculate that they save money in the long run.

Villagers ignore police warnings and police activities in general. The disinterest and disobedience displayed by villagers towards police accurately mirrors their general feelings about the formal state legal apparatus. The perennial struggle over fines and violations around activities that used to be "free" exacerbates the contempt for external authority and makes easy relations between the police and local villagers difficult.

Illegal possession of weapons in a western court could fall within a criminal rather than a civil classification, but no charges would be made for this offense in Shehaam, unless the weapons were flaunted repeatedly and/or such weapons were used in a case of assault or threat. All village households are heavily armed with hand guns, hunting rifles, and automatic weapons. For the local police to attempt to enforce the statute that makes the possession of automatic weapons illegal would be impractical and would further strain their relations within the villages. Rather, the police enforce this statute loosely, interpreting such possession as a civil infraction, unless the weapon is used against another individual.

Another important characteristic of these cases is that police discretion is the predominant variable in deciding whether a warning will be issued, either written or verbal, or whether the individual will be brought directly to the station for questioning and citation. "Public" merely indicates that cases are recorded as matters of public record, in contrast to most of the private village cases discussed in the previous chapter. A more detailed breakdown of the state-initiated public cases from the police records is given in Table 5.2. The analytical categories follow the case headings from the local records as closely as possible.

This statistical breakdown indicates that the use of the external legal apparatus is usually involuntary. People do sometimes choose to go to court, as we will see, but out of context these figures might lead planners to assume that the amount of interaction with the legal system is generated by villagers as active users of the modern legal apparatus. The inside view, however, shows that the state often reaches into the village to pull people into the legal system, but that villagers rarely actively involve themselves in formal legality. Villagers have neither the expertise nor the money to use the courts freely and effectively. The users' perspective in this instance clarifies the real meaning of access to law versus access to redress. There are only two cases on record in 9 years in which the individuals claimed the state as the defendant in a complaint—when the municipality was sued for flood damage to individual property.

The second largest category of state-initiated cases involves hashish, one of the major cash crops in the area. An investigation into these 12 cases revealed that the charges all resulted from factional competitions. In only one such case did the strained relations between a group of farmers and the chief of police lead to formal criminal charges and arrest. In this case, police initiated a blanket complaint against all growers in the area. In Lebanon it is legal to grow hashish, but illegal to harvest or sell it. One man volunteered from among the growers to stand for prosecution for a harvesting charge to lessen political tensions in the village and to begin to negotiate a new status quo with the police. He turned himself over to the police and confessed to the charges stated in the formal complaint. During the years he spend in prison he was paid and his family well taken care of by an alliance of growers in the village. All other crop-related conflicts on record were instigated by political rivals within the village or by regional political bosses. In the other 11 cases, investigations were made and individuals often spent some time in the village jail during these investigations, but the charges were ultimately dropped for lack of evidence.

The production of hashish creates another important element of social control

The Police

TABLE 5.2
State-Initiated Cases[a]

Category	Type of case	Number of cases	Percentage of category	Percentage of total
A	Building without permit	52	87	71
	Illegal sale of tobacco		2	
	Illegal possession of weapons		5	
	Disturbing the peace		2	
	Flour mill without permit		2	
	Block factory without permit		2	
B	Drug peddling	12	33	16
	Illegal planting of hemp		8	
	Hemp smuggling		25	
	Hemp trading		17	
	Illegal possession of hemp		17	
C	Suicide	9	11	13
	Illegal use of public land		22	
	Kidnapping		11	
	Assault with weapons		22	
	Debt collection		11	
	Theft (from public works)		11	
	Illegal manufacture of arms		11	
		73 cases	100%	100%

Table Summary

A   Administrative, civil wrongs
B   Hashish related
C   Criminal wrongs

[a]$N = 73$ cases.

in the central Beqaa Valley. Conflict related to ownership, theft, or damage of this crop cannot be taken to court because it is illegal to sell hashish. This is a strong factor in keeping local economic conflict mediated within the village. Police receive payments to avoid patrols in the fields during harvest season, and this further decreases peoples' respect for them as representatives of the national legal and moral order.

When the administrative and crop-related cases are extracted, all that remain are five cases (in 9 years) that involved publicly defined criminal acts or crimes between persons. These were the illegal manufacture of arms, property damage, theft, debt, assault with weapons, and suicide.

Two factors emerge clearly from the analysis of these police cases: Disputes within the village are infrequently dealt with at this formal level, and disputes between Christians and Moslems were overwhelmingly resolved outside this public arena. The total number of internal village cases (28) is less than half the number of cases recorded in the same period against outsiders (59). Tables 5.3 and 5.4 compare police cases inside the village with cases reaching outside. In both tables the types of disputes are arranged in descending order of frequency.

Christian–Moslem disputes in the sample of "outside" disputes make up 60% of the total cases. Although there is strong pressure to contain and mediate cross-religious disputes inside the village for the sake of on-going relationships, cross-religious disputes with nonresidents are likely to proceed to the formality of police action. Furthermore, 60% of these cross-religious cases outside the village were disputes over scarce resources (Table 5.4, Category A).

Nearly 25% of all these cases against nonresidents of the village were violent crimes against persons (Category B). Follow-up on a number of these cases indicated that physical violence often erupted around a property or resource matter such as the illegal use of property. Such facts were seldom officially recorded. Therefore, it is impossible to calculate exactly how many of these recorded cases were directly related to tangible resources—land, animals, water, and crops. These police cases, combined with the unrecorded, locally mediated cases, indicate that at least two-thirds of all disputes were somehow land- and

TABLE 5.3
Police Cases between Individuals
Inside the Village

Type of case	Number of cases	Percentage of total
Physical assault	28	13
Illegal use of property		13
Theft		11
Personal injury		11
Unauthorized building		11
Suspected theft, search		7
Crop damage		7
Assault with weapons		7
Right of usufruct		4
Property rights		4
Attempted murder		4
Digging without permit		4
Insult		4
		100%

Source: Witty, 1978.

TABLE 5.4
Police Cases between Individuals and Institutions Outside the Village

Category	Type of case	Number of cases	Percentage of category	Percentage of total
A	Property damage	36	26	61
	Theft		19	
	Illegal use of property		19	
	Fraud		14	
	Crop damage		11	
	Forgery		8	
	Opening water pipes		3	
B	Physical assault	15	48	25
	Injury		20	
	Hit and run		13	
	Threat with weapon		7	
	Assault with weapon		7	
	Attempted murder		7	
C	Debt	8	37	14
	Illegal use of public land		24	
	Unauthorized building		13	
	Verbal threat		13	
	Misconduct		13	
		59 cases	100%	100%

Table Summary

A	Dispute involving scarce resources
B	Violent crimes against persons
C	Minor, miscellaneous disputes

Source: Witty, 1978.

crop-related; the remaining disputes were motivated by more diffuse interests of reputation, honor, and power alliances in the village and environs.

A breakdown in frequencies according to an analytical classification of cases for the entire corpus of police records is given in Table 5.5.

Although the cases against outsiders are weighted towards crimes against persons, cases against insiders, and those initiated by the state against insiders, tend to emphasize property disputes. This is consistent with the local political competition over scarce resources that decreases in intensity as relations expand outward into the region. Local cases are more intense because of a high frequency of mediation principles at work in one community, local leadership that encourages a closed economic system, relatively equal status relations within the village, and a high degree of intricate economic and kinship obligations. As each of these

TABLE 5.5
Frequency Breakdown of Total Police Recorded Sample (1965-1973)[a]

Type of case	Number of cases	Classification	Percentage of type	Percentage of total
Illegal use of property	52	Property	17	31
Theft			23	
Property damage			23	
Suspected theft			3	
Forgery			6	
Debt			8	
Illegal use of public property			8	
Digging without permit			2	
Usufruct			2	
			100%	
Physical assault	41	Personal	30	26
Hit and run			7	
Fraud			10	
Suicide			2	
Assault with weapons			17	
Threat			5	
Attempted murder			7	
Kidnapping			2	
Misconduct			2	
Perjury			2	
Injury			16	
			100%	
Building without permit	55	Administrative	80	34
Illegal sale of tobacco			2	
Illegal possession of weapons			8	
Illegal opening of water pipes			2	
Blockade of public road			2	
Disturbing the peace			2	
Business without a permit			4	
			100%	
Trading hemp	12	Crops	17	9
Drug peddling			33	
Illegal possession of hemp			17	
Hemp smuggling			25	
Illegal planting of hemp			8	
			100%	100%

[a] $N = 160$ cases.

factors decreases in intensity as one moves out of village network, relations become more competitive, open, and transactional. Disputes within these types of relationships are more likely to be resolved through intermediation. The overall distribution of cases per type for the 9-year police record sample is, therefore, relatively balanced between personal and property violations.

Understanding the role of police within the village and community is best illustrated by Case 8.

CASE 8. ASSAULT IN THE FIELDS

Albert and Ali had been arguing for some time over grazing rights on a certain piece of land. Ali continually allowed his shepherd to let sheep wander onto land that legally belonged to Albert. Albert had repeatedly told the shepherd that he was trespassing and that the wheat stubble grazing had been promised to someone else.

On this particular day, Albert and several of his relatives were traveling through the fields on a tractor, and Ali's brother, Ahmad, was with them. They came upon Ali on the road, and he motioned for them to stop.

He began to argue with Albert. Ali said that Albert had insulted him by insulting his shepherd and chasing him off the land. Ali continued by saying that he felt that Albert was being very high-handed in his dealings with his neighbors.

The argument became heated, and without warning, Ali pulled a pistol from his garment and told Albert he was going to shoot him. Ahmad struck his brother's arm. The pistol discharged but Albert was unharmed because the bullet was deflected. Everyone was enraged, and Ahmad quickly led his brother away so there would be no further trouble. Ali left reluctantly, still shouting, cursing, and swearing to kill Albert when he saw him again.

When they returned from the fields later that afternoon, Albert and his relatives were still angry and concerned about Albert's welfare. After hours of family discussion, several men went with Albert to the police station in Shehaam and reported the shooting incident.

Ali could not be found, and his brother was called to testify. Ahmad swore that he had not even been in the fields that day, and that he knew nothing of the incident. He had not seen Ali for several days and did not know where he could be found.

One aspect of the involvement of the local police is the deterrent effect of public reporting. Filing a public complaint is one method of containing a dispute or putting opponents temporarily off-balance. By using the threat of actual arrest and police involvement, Albert wanted to have this particular incident resolved quickly. Albert explained that by publicly announcing the attempt on his life, Ali's family would be forced to take some kind of immediate conciliatory action.

Ali's brother, Ahmad, reported that upon hearing that a formal complaint had been filed, the elders of the family called a meeting. It was decided that Ali would remain hidden for another day while negotiations were begun with Albert's family. Ali's family agreed that he had done a foolish thing, and the family felt obligated to apologize, even though they had supported Ali in the original grazing dispute.

Ahmad explained that because the matter had been officially recorded, his family wished to finish the matter and remove it from the public arena as soon as possible; this action, they felt could keep Ali out of trouble, lessen the tension between the two families, and salvage their family honor. Formal charges are frequently dropped if mediation is proceeding. In this case, Albert was free to return to the police station and say that he had exaggerated his original story in the heat of anger, or that he had been mistaken in the identity of his assailant. There would be no further charges or investigations and the case would be closed as "dropped for lack of evidence."

The police have the capability to function as conciliatory agents in local communities. Administratively they are not limited to enforcement, formal investigation, and reporting. Villagers tell of a previous police chief and a time when relations between the police and the community were friendly. Formal complaints tended to be resolved inside the village during that period. The personality of the police chief is clearly a determining factor in the way the police view their role in the community. An emphasis on mediation, rather than routine enforcement, allows the police flexibility in their task of containment, villagers say, and brings them more respect as well. The bustling officiality of police operations often heightens tensions in the village: Police have searched homes without the presence of a mayor, arrested and held elderly relatives when a young violator could not be found, and sided with a policeman in a dispute with a village youth. These types of actions, villagers argue, signal that the police cannot be trusted in daily village affairs, let alone in times of crisis.

The dispute between the village youth and a local policeman described in Chapter 6 (see page 98) further illustrates some of the tensions between police and local residents, and the kinds of tensions and verbal encounters that lead to disputes and sustained hard feelings.

The police chief remembered by villagers with respect considered himself a mediator, informants say, and personally involved himself in disputes in the community under his jursidiction, preferring that disputes be informally resolved. This former police chief was also a Druze and, therefore, not aligned with any of the religious groups found in Shehaam.

The current police chief is a Shia Moslem and this limits his ability to act as a neutral mediator—half of the village does not trust him to be impartial. The Moslem community also does not hold the police chief in high regard because of his unwillingness to acknowledge village leadership, overlook certain infractions, reduce fines for villagers charged with permit violations, and refrain from interfering in disputes if that is the wish of the parties.

The police role and function in the village is one of tenuous authority and enforcement of local codes. Choosing to call the police threatens an opponent with escalation of a case and applies pressure to a case that is moving slowly or going badly locally. External institutions like the police can be rallied as one type of personal strategy. Another external institution that is manipulated the same way is the court system.

The Courts

Police cases overwhelmingly involved villagers with persons from outside Shehaam. Of the 28 police cases between local villagers, only two could not be mediated. These cases both involved payments of long-term debts in which family ties had seriously eroded, and the complainant had no desire to continue kin or economic relations with the debtors. The parties were related through marriage rather than birth, and this factor also made the kin relationship easier to sever. In both cases the plaintiffs were alone and without large families as well, and this increased their perceived need for monetary gain and security. Generally, although a court sentence is not considered legitimate punishment because it is external to community values, this attitude is changing. Villagers admit that people are sometimes willing to rely on the court to punish or correct a person's behavior. This is particularly true in cases of the type just described, and property damage cases when clear monetary gain is involved. With the formal leverage of a court on their sides, plaintiffs have an easier time collecting unpaid debts because they can threaten to use the courts repeatedly and have the debtor returned to jail if the payments are not completed.

Parties may also threaten to take a case directly to court and bypass local mediation because this is sometimes effective in moving opponents who are slow to reconcile.

More frequently, complaints are made to the police or courts in order to push a dispute into a higher level of formality: This makes one's anger clear and public and requires one's opponents to abandon the defendant or take definite action to settle the dispute.

The threat of police or court involvement to publicly escalate a conflict usually functions in a reverse fashion to initiate or speed up the mediation process; threatening to use the court usually insures that the court will not be required to make the final decision. In cases of clear monetary gain where the defendant is stubborn, hostile, or unimportant to the complainant, the records as well as villagers' attitudes show an increasing willingness to really use the courts. Such use requires a certain amount of capital to initiate a case (about $150) and until free legal services are widely available this option will rest primarily with the landowners and wealthy.

Attitudes and Conflicting Jurisdictions

Mediation is highly developed in Shehaam because the principles of conciliatory agreements are strong and pervasive in the village and the society at large. The values of mediation are particularly strong locally, as the theory of mediation would predict. In a case of accidental death to a child who was struck by a villager's car, the dead child's father refused the payment offered for her death because there was no negligence involved on the part of the driver. Villagers cite this case as an example of the integrity and honor that must be maintained within a local community. The formal legal system would require that damage be paid in such a case and would perhaps imprison the offender. Such a punishment would not be just, villagers say, because it is not what the two involved parties agreed was just and honorable conduct in this case.

To elaborate this point, it is important to understand the distinctions that villagers and courts make between public and private rights (see Corfu, 1951). *Public rights* are those rights that derive from and accrue to the state and its legal system. Public rights originate in the Lebanese civil and criminal codes and are administered and enforced through the police and courts. When there is a breach of statuatory law, that breach must be corrected by the authority of the state. Under this authority, if one man kills another, he is tried and sentenced to a minimum of 15 months and a maximum of 7 years in prison.

Private rights, in such a homicide case, would involve the right of payment that would be made in compensation by the killer's family to the victim's family. Community members believe that these rights should not be decided by the courts, but between the families themselves, with the help of mediators. Private rights originate from among the people, are relevant only between individuals and families, and are derived from community norms.

An example of individual choice between exercising private and public rights was recounted as follows: If a man has two sons and one son kills the other, the father has two choices. He may initiate a case aginst his son and file a formal accusation and complaint. The court will try his son and sentence him. Thus, both the public and private rights present in the case are recognized. If the father does not initiate a court case against his son, but the police discover the crime and initiate formal action, the son is also tried and sentenced to jail. This, however, is an exercise of the public rights involved in the act of murder and does not resolve private-right obligations.

The formal legal system makes a clear distinction between these two types of rights, but sees both as legitimately deriving from the authority of the legal system

Attitudes and Conflicting Jurisdictions

and the power of the constitution. It is the authority of the courts and judicial administrators to decide both issues at all levels of jurisdiction.

Villagers recognize the power and authority of the state to enforce its laws and statutes. Private rights, villagers feel, are not the proper and legitimate jurisdiction of the state. Court officials and lawyers do not live in the village or region as neighbors, coworkers, and political competitors; they have no local social relations based on kinship or political alliance. Therefore, villagers feel that any "neutral" decisions that courts, lawyers, and judges make with regard to private relationships and rights between villagers are uninformed and inappropriate.

Another reason not to use the courts, the people of Shehaam argue, is that rules of evidence are too restricted within formal court proceedings. The social history of the case, which they feel bears directly on questions of premediation, fault, obligation, and community standards of reasonable behavior, is not allowed to be developed in sufficient depth or detail. Pleadings are subject to various interpretations and consequences within the legal system and require the technical expertise of a lawyer. Unless they are relatives or dependable members of one's political network, lawyers are generally uninterested in the social and political implications of a case, and they also charge prohibitive fees for litigation or office consultation.

Rules of fault in accident or injury, particularly with regard to the concept of negligence are different in customary practice and legal philosophy. Local standards value the life of the social group more highly than they value one individual life, in the sense that social groups are perpetuated and saved needless retribution killings by the compensation for one life. Napoleonic legal philosophy and the French law that was adapted to Lebanese use values each individual life separate from the larger social group, and takes the protection of each individual under its authority and jurisdiction.

Many villagers feel that if they lose the option to actively choose between alternatives, they will be at a competitive disadvantage against those who have the influence, money, and time to pursue a case through the legal system. Even political brokers, as we will see in Chapter 6, have a difficult time waging long, drawn out legal battles in the courts with businesses, banks, or wealthy individuals. Usually extensive cases are not worth the time and trouble for both villagers or political leaders. Case 9 will illustrate this point more clearly.

CASE 9. THE CASE OF THE INJURED WORKER

An elderly man from Shehaam is the sole support of an extended household. This household consists of two unmarried sisters, two daughters-in-law (one widowed, one pregnant and divorced), and several small children.

The man, Abdallah, is sick and unable to work; he is 85 years old. Including himself, there are nine individuals in this household who need support.

The family derives a small income from their sheep (milk, wool, etc.), but this income is seasonal and quite variable. His married son Ali worked for a foundry in Beirut and used to be the sole support of this household. Ali worked for this company for 6 years, and then left after a dispute with the director. After several months, Ali returned to the director and requested his job back. The director agreed, but said Ali would lose the 6 years credit to his social security insurance (diman al-ijtima'ti).

Ali agreed to these terms and returned to work. He worked for another 6 years before he was injured. A piece of iron fell on him at the factory and he was hospitalized. The foundry did not report the accident, but the family reported it later to the police in the municipality where the accident had occurred. Ali was released from the hospital after 8 days, but died 3 days later at home; he was 36 years old.

The insurance administration refused to pay the family compensation. The accident was not reported by the employer, the family reported the accident several days after it occurred, and whether the death was directly related to the injury was uncertain.

This case required a lawyer who was willing to fight a lengthy debate in the courts for very little immediate remuneration. It required free legal aid. Abdallah's household had few political or factional allies within the village and his external ties were weak because of his long absence from active political life. He had relied on his healthy sons for support, but now they were both dead (the other son died in the army in 1967). In such a case, an individual without strong, traditional support networks is isolated from legal representation. Abdallah felt that he had a strong and proper case against the government, the social security insurance administration, and the foundry, but he had no one who was willing to support him in this legal and political struggle. He had consulted several lawyers, but each had told him that they needed $200 to begin to investigate the case. The household's annual income was less than $200. Legal redress through formal channels was out of reach in this case.

This case is unusual because most individuals' support networks are more active and extensive than Abdallah's. If a younger man had a similar problem and had not been confined to the house in sickness for many years, he would be able to reach relatives or powerful political brokers to have the legal fees waived or reduced as personal favors.

Abdallah's case is *not* unusual, however, in the sense that such disputes involving unequal power sources will predictably become more frequent for villagers. Families are dispersed through employment outside the villages, and large, powerful governmental and business concerns are becoming more active in the rural areas of the country. The increasing political awareness of some of the younger population is also beginning to change the power and structure of the external political networks radiating from the village as we will see in the next chapter. As individuals become more issue-oriented and unobligated to traditional power relations, political leaders will be less willing to provide counsel and intermediation, which Abdallah needed, to individuals who do not have proven alliances to their political spheres.

This chapter has focused on the police and the courts and their practical use in the daily lives of Shehaam's villagers. Mediation sometimes does not work, particularly in cases where monetary gain is clear and where one of the disputing parties has no wish to continue a social relationship with the other. Mediation sometimes requires indirect measures to pressure a person to reconcile, which the family may be unwilling or unable to do. In such cases, again involving relatively unnegotiable sums of money or property, the value of threatening to initiate police or court involvement is high. Mediation also will not be effective when the wealth and status between two parties is extreme and unnegotiable. In such instances, people need the courts, lawyers, and police to work for their benefit. Such a proactive functioning of the legal system is nonexistent in Shehaam, and villagers continue to rely heavily on themselves, their relatives, and powerful regional political leaders.

The problems of rapid social change, an economically stratified society, and the juxtaposition of two culturally different legal systems are common to most developing nations. The village view of progress, development, and economic survival raises certain implications for the future of the countryside and the nation that call for a discussion of regional politics, leadership, and access to influence in dealing with bureaucracies, government institutions, powerful individuals, and businesses.

6

The Waasta-Makers: Intermediation

When mediation fails, or is ineffective because of extreme status differences between disputants, political brokers are relied upon by the villagers to exert influence and use their own power to equalize the status relationships and find a workable remedy for villagers' problems. The influence bargaining system is ubiquitous, and every villager has at least one broker or patron to rely on in time of need. This influence system is an extension of the political networks within each village, but also ties directly into the economic relations within the Beqaa Valley region. Politics, disputing, farming, and economic success are all regionally enmeshed in a reciprocal and relatively closed patronage system.

Political Brokers: The Waasta-Makers

The relationship between village-based support networks and external influence networks is complementary—personal networks are focused on village factional politics and external networks are geared to reach outside the village to people in positions of power. Personal support networks are more often organized around individuals working toward specific goals. External networks are usually activated by individuals acting through the family. Any individual may activate links in the external network to which he or she has access in order to achieve a particular end, but those political links were founded and traditionally bound by the family as the central unit of production, leadership, and political action. Political brokers traditionally deal with families as groups, not with individuals acting independent of, or in opposition to, the family structure. The character of these traditional service, patron–client ties is changing, however. Transactional, reciprocal business relations exist in external networks and appear to be increasing in frequency. Some individuals are beginning to view external political relations as issue-oriented types of alliances.

Intermediation, influence bargaining, or the *waasta*, is used to gain access to political resources outside the village support networks. Traditionally, political brokers (or *waasta-makers*) are not members of the village community, but men whose support networks are centered in historical family leadership patterns, wealth, national political careers, and patronage relations extending to several family and village groups within the region. Such men are large land owners, professional politicians in or out of office, wealthy businessmen, and often they are descendents of tribal ancestors who ruled the region for centuries, even under Ottoman occupation.

Villagers' external influence networks connect them to such men of influence to counsel and intermediate in times of crisis. The politically astute family will manipulate the external intermediation system better than their neighbors and political opponents. Villagers argue, however, that there is good and bad influence.

Influence itself is a neutral factor and its uses vary depending on the morality of people's choices. Informants frequently cited employment as an illustration of good and bad *waasta* or intermediation. For example, an individual from Shehaam could study very hard and become better educated than any of her or his family elders. Often such individuals are unable to find jobs and a good *waasta* will find such an individual a job. Under the same set of circumstances, an uneducated and unqualified person could get the same job instead of the educated individual through strong political influence, and this is a commonly cited example of a bad *waasta*.

Sometimes a *waasta* may even override a legal decision from the courts. A villager may be sentenced to 10 years in jail, but will serve only 2 years before he or she is released. Whether or not such a *waasta* is considered good or bad depends on whether the formal judicial punishment coincides with villagers' principles of obligations, payment, and redress.

Political brokers have regional networks that are dense and interconnected; they all know one another personally or by reputation. By acting as liaisons between villagers and higher level decision makers, waasta-makers work locally to maintain support relationships with villagers and to provide villagers with services. At the same time they manipulate higher level relationships, in competition with other brokers, in order to develop a network of strategic channels to key political resources (decision makers, bureaucrats, national politicians, cabinet ministers, judges, judicial administrators, attorneys). Because of their political backgrounds, brokers have access to powerful decision makers in the various agencies, administrations, and higher echelons of government whether or not they are holding an active office. The broker's expansive networks link villages to a regional and national system that can be used to obtain services that are unavailable in the village. Such outside services may be sought in order to influence or threaten individuals inside the village, but brokers try to avoid this kind of situation because influence becomes complicated by local factional alliances.

Political brokers do not immediately and continually break rules and provide favors for individuals who seek their assistance. They initially try to reconcile and, if necessary, mediate between conflicting opinions and points of view. Often a broker will be successful at this conciliatory level and will not need to apply influence elsewhere. According to the villagers, the successful balance of conciliation and political power is the mark of a true waasta-maker.

The broker's range of influence is territorial and based in part on traditional, long-standing ties of support and alliance between his family and families in the area. As with the concept of community, a broker's area of influence is not geographically defined, but is defined as a social area of historical and on-going relationships. Areas of political influence are not mutually exclusive territories, therefore, and many brokers draw followers and supporters from the same regions. There are five such political brokers in the Beqaa area with influence in Shehaam. In election years, the brokers' political activities in the rural areas increase in order to reaffirm and consolidate their political ties. Visits are made to villages, villagers are sought out as they work in the fields, subsequent coffee and social interaction revolve around political and economic issues, and brokers generally make themselves visible, useful, and helpful to their constituents. Villagers know that an election year is a particularly good time to ask for an important or difficult *waasta*, for the chances of success are extremely good. During elections, villagers say, the brokers count on the votes of their traditional "following" in the village communities, either for themselves personally or for the candidate who has their backing.

Traditional patron–client ties are beginning to change in character. Brokers are no longer automatically able to draw on local support. Families, as well as individuals, are beginning to become more selective with their political affiliations and support. The old networks are becoming more flexible, and political action is emerging as a new focal point for community support. Issues such as consumer prices, wages, imported labor, and crop pricing and distribution are emerging as the kinds of economic issues that will rally political supporters around a leader. Such shifts in political priorities were clearly emerging in the early 1970s, and individual villagers, particularly politically active young males, were trying to politicize their families and village elders. Dissent continued to grow, patron–client relations were subject to realignment after years of family allegiance, and the most politically active marched in the streets of a local market town protesting rising sugar and flour prices, lack of government supervision, control of sugar hoarders, and the lack of government action in dealing with these condidtions of privation and hardship. Several young men from Shehaam participated in that demonstration. They were criticized, individually and as a group, by several local political brokers and elites. This verbal chastisement, the lack of action against the intolerable conditions among farmers, and continued support of the traditional status quo within the country gradually lost those local brokers support among villagers. The long-term effects are still developing, but individuals in the village are increasingly aware that their political alternatives are not as limited and traditionally bound as they once were.

A typical role for a political broker is illustrated in Case 10. Secondarily, the role of police is further expanded. The Moslem family involved in this case needed an intermediator between themselves, the village police, and the regional judicial administration in Baalbek.

CASE 10. A FISTFIGHT WITH A POLICEMAN

One of the local policemen was passing through town on the way to a neighborhood store. Members of the boy's family contend that the policeman had been drinking and was going to the shop for more Arak, but this could not be proved.

When passing through town, he came upon a group of young men, greeted them, and shook hands with some of them. One of the youths, Sam, did not want to shake hands and refused to do so. The policeman left.

On his return from the shop (with a brown bag wrapped around what appeared to be a bottle), he confronted Sam and demanded to know why he had not returned his greeting. He grabbed the youth by the shirt and asked if he needed a big kick to return his greeting.

Sam replied that as far as he was concerned, the policeman had no business speaking to him that way.

Sam: "I'm free to answer or refuse."
Policeman: "Did I ever tell you to eat a donkey prick?"
Sam: "No."
Policeman: "Well, I'm telling you now."
Sam: "I respect the uniform you're wearing, or I would beat your ass."
Policeman: "I'm not hiding behind this uniform, you worm."

With this he motioned the youth aside. He then drew his pistol, and Sam fled up the street; his friends and witnesses followed.

The policeman followed up another street and intercepted Sam at an intersection.

Thinking he might shoot him, Sam said later, he picked up a large rock and threw it at the policeman; the policeman was hit in the head and

Political Brokers: The Waasta-Makers

temporarily lost his balance. Sam grabbed him by his arms, trying to get the pistol, and urged his friends to help him accomplish this. A fight developed in which Sam used another rock to hit the policeman on the side of the head.

Spectators arrived on the scene and separated the two. The policeman was bleeding and injured, but not seriously. Sam fled the scene.

When Sam could not be found in the village, the local police called in armed reinforcements from a nearby police station. This station called the district office in Baalbek and a small group of army infantry were also dispatched to Shehaam. These forces were searching the village for the youth and his family's house was virtually under seige by armed forces of various types. Villagers felt that this was an overreaction to a local fistfight and an inappropriate display of force.

Sam's family felt that there were two sides to the argument between their son and the policeman, but the case had escalated so quickly beyond the village that they were afraid the youth would not get a fair hearing. They were also afraid that the youth would be beaten by the police if they released him to police custody. In this circumstance, the youth remained hidden by his family, and several male elders from the family went immediately (late the same evening) to the home of a political broker who had helped them in times of crisis before; he lived in a nearby town.

The broker, Michael, after hearing all the details of the case and its development over the past hours, made a phone call to the District Attorney of Baalbek; he did not know the District Attorney personally, but they had many friends in common, and they knew each other officially by reputation. Michael explained the situation to the District Attorney and asked him if he would do something about removing the extra armed soldiers and police who had been called into Shehaam. Michael explained that the youth's uncles and father were with him at that moment, and he conveyed their side of the argument as well as their fears for the youth's safety at the hands of the police. Michael explained that the family was willing to bring the youth directly to the court in Baalbek as soon as the armed reinforcements were removed from the village.

After some discussion, Michael agreed to accompany the youth and his family to meet with the District Attorney in Baalbek the next morning. Michael gave his word of honor that the youth would appear before the court. The District Attorney agreed to call the army commander in Baalbek and have him recall the reinforcements.

These actions were all accomplished early the next morning and the case was ultimately resolved in a military court in Beirut (because Sam was a member of the army reserves). The case was dismissed by that court on the basis of good character witnesses on the youth's behalf; Michael was one of the witnesses who testified on Sam's behalf. The court issued the youth a stern warning and he was able to return to the village after having been in custody 2 nights in Baalbek and 3 nights in Beirut. Although this particular dispute was ultimately resolved to everyone's satisfaction, this family's relations with the local police continued to be strained and unfriendly.

Political brokers often provide such alternatives to local court and police proceedings. Such alternatives are, like mediation, less costly, more flexible, and more efficient than the formal legal system.

Economic Relations and Regional Integration

Economic relations are also bound within these changing political networks. Brokers are often directly involved in the purchase of regional crops, but if they are not, they provide buyers and middlemen for the farmers in their area. Since every family in Shehaam traditionally has access to one or more brokers, they can choose between buyers.

Shehaam and the surrounding community subsist on a mixed cash crop, subsistence farming, and a small percentage of unskilled labor (tinkers, stone masons, plumbers, metal workers, farm laborers). One cash crop, sunflowers, is sold directly to the government for a set price. Wheat and hashish, however, are sold through local market towns and private buyers. Price bargaining is the responsibility of each individual farmer. Using the local markets requires a great deal of comparative knowledge to get premium prices for the year's harvest. Most farmers in Shehaam prefer to negotiate with private buyers so they can perpetuate stable economic relations over a number of years; this is particularly true for the hashish crop. Establishing relations with a specific buyer increases farmers' security, they feel, because they can count on selling their entire yield and bargaining for competitive prices. Maintaining particular economic ties over a number of years gives a farmer more social latitude and precedent with which to bargain.

Each year during the spring (for wheat) and summer (for hashish) regional buyers arrive in the valley to make contacts. They are interested in surveying the crops, reestablishing ties with former clients, and finding new clients. The buyers are responsible for marketing the crops; they have business networks with bakeries, mills, and food production companies with regard to the wheat, and foreign markets with regard to the hashish. Farmers can, however, independently find local markets for their wheat and garden vegetables, and often do.

Strategies for finding and maintaining buyers and business associates is part of the local political process as it extends outside the boundaries of the village. In addition to the family networks that establish kinship ties outside the village, each family has ties to powerful political individuals. Kin networks may sometimes be used to reach these men, but usually regional political ties are based on transactional ties of reciprocity or the obligations of a patron-client relationship. These personal external networks integrate villagers into the larger political and economic system.

Often political and economic ties are so closely associated at the regional level that to sever one is to sever the other. This is a risk and a cost that must be weighed seriously by any farmer who wishes to negotiate with buyers of his choice from another area. If the traditional basis for economic relations changes, farmers will increasingly look for buyers and better prices elsewhere.

The economic and political relationships involved in these marketing transactions are important because of the constraints they apply to the villagers' use of formal legal agencies, and the access to the political system that they provide. The political nature of economic relations combined with the problems of marketing an illegal cash crop create interlocking systems of social control at the regional level. Conflicts involving illegal cash crops cannot be made widely known due to discretion and care in dealing with the police, and they cannot be taken to court precisely because they are illegal. This leaves villagers few alternatives to remaining bound within the regional networks of patronage and power. There is a great deal of protection and dependence built into the patron–client aspects of these political networks. Not only are economic disputes mediated and resolved within this intermediation network, but the network also protects individual farmers from the police and the legal hazards of transporting the crop. Since hashish is a very productive and lucrative cash crop, the incidence of theft and destruction between village competitors is high. Farmers collectively hire several watchmen as the crops begin to mature, but farmers need protection, redress, and access to men of influence if more serious or prolonged trouble involving crops does arise.

Villagers report a serious incident in which economic networks were divided and weakened by a dispute, protection broke down, and local police plowed under large quantities of hashish shortly before harvest. Protection against such hazards and risks is an important function of the intermediation and social control system that connects the village to regional political authority.

Other kinds of risks are also involved in such a system. Protection from the vicissitudes of local and personal politics is hard for the farmer to calculate. If one's broker is angered, for example, not only does conflict arise, but a farmer may be effectively cut off from necessary services and support channels. Even temporary political isolation can be detrimental to economic and political survival.

Women in Intermediation

Women are not publicly involved in economic dealings and business transactions. Families expand their regional political networks, however, in the same way they expand their family centered networks. The external political ties a woman brings to a marriage are as strong and extensive as those of a man. Women advise men in their extended family and household on the character and reputation of various brokers and elites. Women assess political figures astutely because they have access to varied information channels in the course of their everyday work and travels throughout the fields. Through their interaction with other women, and the women of the political leaders' extended households, village women collect a wealth of personal, political, and economic information. A man and wife often jointly visit a broker's or buyer's household and later confer about their combined impressions of the man, his resources, and his intentions.

Furthermore, women are able to draw from a wide variety of political experiences, for they are not only aware of their husband's political networks and supporters, but often have intimate knowledge of their mother's and father's political networks as well. In this sense, women contribute considerable political knowledge and expertise to the family unit, even though they do not publicly involve themselves in negotiations and economic transactions with political elites. The inclusion and active use of women's extensive political information adds depth and diversity to a family's political standing in the community and insures the success of economic alliances within the region.

Conclusions

Recognition of the situation that exists in villages such as Shehaam is the first step in understanding national legal development. Lawyers, judges, and administrators assume that villagers are integrated into the national legal system because they see them in courts. They do not seek the reasons villagers are there, or worry that individuals with a network of political alliances throughout the country seldom choose to use the court system.

The role of women, as well as the role of men, in the legal and political process in the village and region is an area that must be pursued in greater depth (see Beck and Keddie, 1978; Boserup, 1970; Rosaldo and Lamphere, 1974). It has been shown in many geographic areas that the structure of factional networks and the politics of factional competition must also be clearly understood (Bailey, 1969, 1971; Boissevain, 1974; Epstein, 1974) before attempting to assess or predict the larger political systems. The political and economic networks that bind villagers to the region and the government must be given serious attention because they affect the villagers' perceptions of values, jursidictions, community solidarity, and justice.

Villagers in the central Beqaa area of Lebanon have modified their traditional process of dispute settlement (mediation) and conflict management (networks and intermediation) to take account of the presence of formal legal structures. These villagers have *not* been successfully assimilated into the procedures or, more importantly, they have not accepted the legal principles upon which the formal legal system rests. Rather, they have incorporated the formal system of courts, judges, police, and prisons into their own local practices. Some conces-

Conclusions

sions have been made locally to recognize the state's jurisdiction to prosecute crimes, but this recognition represents a concession to power rather than an acceptance of legitimate legal authority.

If village mediation is more supportive, more satisfying, and less costly than the formal legal system, villagers will continue to mediate disputes internally. If the regional systems of economic support, alliance, and protection are necessary to the villagers' economic and political survival, and if they need such systems to compete with other farmers and educate their children to be competitive and successful in a rapidly changing world, regional intermediation networks will continue to be more effective than national courts in resolving villagers' legal, political, and social problems.

People do not automatically use legal systems just because they are there. They have specific personal, political, and legal reasons for using them. The poor and powerless often cannot use a formal legal system to their own advantage. They have neither the technical knowledge nor the money that facilitates access to such systems.

As the theory of mediation notes, formal definitions of crimes and jurisdictions must be synonymous with or complementary to the informal definitions that make up the social and legal world of the users. Without such overlap and consistency, the formal legitimacy of a legal system will not transcend the indigenous values of the people who use that system.

The general principles of mediation are well developed and clearly identified in Shehaam. People prefer to use village and regional mechanisms for settling disputes because they have the knowledge necessary to use these mechanisms to their advantage, and these mechanisms are also more efficient, more participatory, more satisfying, and more accessible. The interwoven relationships in the community make mediation a very workable form of conflict management. The limits of mediation, the constraints of the economic system, and the problem of access to the courts make intermediation on the part of elites a necessary form of redress and equalization.

The courts should not be made more accessible just because they are there, but because they understand and complement local mediational systems and empower individuals to protect and sustain personal freedoms.

Some documentation of economic development programs (Kanaan, 1972) and the position of villagers in regional economic organization (Doumani, 1974; Witty, 1978) has been done in Lebanon. Information accumulated about a particular village and region can have significant impact if analyzed within the theory of mediation and applied to planned change within the legal system. The information also has applied comparative value in terms of thinking about the American legal system and the American experience of legal institutions, needs, and expectations.

The theory of mediation is a cross-cultural paradigm that requires close investigation of local community political and legal organization. The theory posits relationships between people, mediation, and adjudication that are valid cross-culturally, and which impact uniformly on the use or implementation of mediation in any community within any legal order. Lebanon and the Middle East in general have some of the most well-developed mediation processes documented. This is because local and regional leadership patterns have remained decentralized and viable within local communities, community production and reciprocity systems are closely linked, and the principles of mediation are traditionally strong and supported throughout the social system. To illustrate the reliability of the theoretical propositions of the theory of mediation, and to make a cross-cultural comparison of mediation processes, Chapter 7 describes a successful mediation program in an urban American setting.

7
Mediation in Urban America

Community mediation as a viable and institutionalized alternative to court adjudication in modern societies is a matter of some controversy. The theory of mediation argues that mediation can exist effectively in any social setting when certain predictive conditions are met, but the debate over the viability of mediation in modern urban societies, particularly America, is a predictable one.

Some scholars argue that the fragmented and anonymous social environment of American cities and suburbs precludes sustained personal interaction or participation in community programs. While it may be true that the level of conflict and dispute avoidance in American society is high, the social and personal costs of such avoidance are still being calculated (Danzig and Lowy, 1974, 1975; Felstiner, 1974; Hirshmann, 1970). Felstiner (1974), for example, argues that "adjudication and mediation of... disputes will be hard to institutionalize and avoidance will carry significantly lower costs [p. 82]." He goes to say that:

> Institutionalized mediation of interpersonal disputes will also be infrequent in a TCRS (technologically complex, rich society)... where role differentiation is intense, [and] few persons are qualified by experience to mediate any disputes: everybody's role set is too specialized to be common experience with a significant number of potential disputants... [p. 83].

This argument seriously underestimates the personal costs, such as frustration and powerlessness, associated with the lack of responsive remedy agents (Danzig and Lowy, 1975; Lerner, 1979). It also runs counter to the theory of mediation and the urban ethnographic data which argue that people can and will take action in the face of distance from the law, high personal costs, and conflict (Clowand and Piven, 1977; U.S. LEAA, 1978). Theory posits that mediation in any society grows out of an individual's awareness of his or her community and a need to control one's social and political life within that community. Communities need not be homogenous or kin-related for people to recognize social strengths and weaknesses and work toward changing the causes of conflict. Mediation deals with the causes of conflict, while courts tend to deal with the symptoms of conflict in the form of broken rules.

Sarat (1977), in a review of public opinion studies related to courts, notes that "courts are not particularly visible or salient to the American people. The level of public awareness and knowledge of courts, court personnel, and court decisions is quite low [p. 438]." Even courts that were ostensibly organized to give citizens a local, responsive forum to redress personal grievances evolved into forums for business, government, and utility companies to pursue, and litigate against individual citizens (Yngvesson and Hennessey, 1975).

Mayhew (1975) has further reminded us of the gap between legal needs and legal institutions:

> Whether any given situation becomes defined as a "legal" problem, or, even if so defined, makes its way to an attorney or other agency for possible aid or redress, is a consequence of the social organization of the legal system and the organization of the larger society—including shifting currents of social ideology, the available legal machinery, and the channels for bringing perceived injustices to legal agencies [p. 404].

This tenuous relationship between individuals and their legal institutions is one of the five predictive components of successful mediation.

The following discussion presents a brief profile of one urban American community mediation program. All the premises and principles of successful mediation operate within this program. The community population is urban and racially heterogeneous, and there is a district court in the community that formally should dispose of community conflict and contention. This discussion is presented as a case study for comparison with the Lebanese mediation materials. The program is not specifically identified for purposes of privacy and confidentiality.

The success of mediation within this program largely speaks for itself, and begins to concretely answer theoretical questions about mediation in a complex, urban setting such as those hypothesized succinctly by Danzig and Lowy (1975):

> We think it will be valuable to experiment with forums of mediation for everyday disputes in this country. If a mediator can serve as a third party who is neither coercive nor threatening, litigants may be encouraged to themselves think about the root causes of their disputes, and beyond this about the role social organization plays in causing, defining, and resolving such matters. The process of disputing might become an educational process. Decentralized citizen mediation then, might lead to alterations

in the conventional meanings of bringing a dispute to the police, courts, or local political leaders [pp. 691-692].

The following program is a clear, time-tested case of community mediation in an institutionalized form functioning successfully in coordination with, and complementary to, the district court system.

An Urban Mediation Program

The mediation program described here is one of several community mediation programs operating in the United States. The programs exhibit a range of third-party resolution techniques. The U.S. Law Enforcement Assistance Administration (1978) notes that

> Third-party intervention strategies vary widely from techniques in which the third party simply attempts to facilitate communication to highly structured formal procedures in which the third party is vested with authority by the state to impose a binding resolution upon the parties to the dispute [p. 10].

Mediation is the predominant settlement mode in these projects, however, and all these projects deal with both civil and criminal cases. These projects serve a broad spectrum of the population and mediate a wide range of matters. Some serve a range of people, but limit themselves to highly specific disputes (consumer projects, warranty programs); still others provide services to a limited spectrum of the population, but will mediate a wide range of matters (e.g., Chinese and Jewish community mediation boards); and, some projects serve both a small group of people and deal with only a limited range of issues (e.g., institutional grievance programs) (U.S. LEAA, 1978, pp. 11-12).

The program discussed here serves as urban, predominantly working-class Black and Irish-Catholic population. The Irish Catholics are second- and third-generation immigrant families who have raised themselves out of the older white urban tenements. This population is bracing against Blacks and Puerto Ricans who are entering their community in an effort to escape the mounting problems of the inner city. It is a violent and turbulent community; crime and tension in the area are high and the crime rate continues to rise. The court itself is one of the busiest in the state with some 15,000 criminal cases per year in the early 1970s and the presiding judge is committed to a broad definition of justice and community service.

In this setting all civil, criminal, and small claims complaints must be initiated in the court clerk's office. These complaints are recorded by a male police officer who screens the complaints, most of which are from women he knows by their first names because of the frequency of their visits. It is his discretionary job to make sure the complaint is in proper order, that it is filed in the correct jurisdiction, and that any physical injury or other evidence is noted correctly at the time of the complaint. He also uses his discretionary powers to advise complainants of their rights and duties, and counsels them as to what they may or may not expect the clerk or judge to do, and what they might do to expedite their case before it comes to a hearing (find witnesses, get a medical report, etc.).

The clerk reviews these daily complaints and sets a court date or schedules the conflict for al preliminary hearing. The clerk holds a hearing on interpersonal disputes every afternoon; he explains the law, counsels individuals on appropriate behavior, and tries to get parties to agree on what was reasonable or unreasonable behavior in the dispute. Some cases are disposed of in this way, while nearly an equal portion prefer to continue to a formal court hearing. If both parties to a complaint do not appear, it is assumed that the conflict is resolved, and it is dropped. When only one party appears, the clerk may dismiss the case, continue it at a later date, or issue an arrest warrant; the choice is discretionary and depends on the history of the parties, the history of the case, and the seriousness of the complaint.

THE SETTING

The mediation program was implemented by funneling cases from the intake policeman and the clerk. Months later, the district attorney was added as a referral source, and finally cases began to be referred directly from the court. The case referral mechanisms developed over several months. This period functioned to let the mediation staff get used to one another, and to give the community mediators a chance to begin with a light schedule of cases. Cases include both misdemeanors and felonies, covering such problems as breaking and entering, assault and battery, petty theft, robbery, attempted murder, disturbing the peace, vicious dogs, public nuisance, and debt.

When a referral is made from any source, the program staff is called and a member goes directly to the complainant to explain the mediation process. Participation in the mediation program is voluntary and complainants sign a statement of voluntary participation before a mediation date is set. It is difficult to accurately gauge the indirect pressure that judges, district attorneys, and court clerks may imply to people, but the discussion of the program with a staff member is intended to minimize coercion. People do choose not to mediate, and this offers evidence that participation is self-determined and voluntary.

The mediation program is located in a storefront office one block from the courthouse. The program has a small, busy staff that does intake interviews and explains the program in the courthouse and in the office, schedules mediation sessions, handles social service referrals, follows up on mediated cases at 2-week and 3-month intervals, and coordinates the community resources with the individual needs of the complainants.

The idea behind the mediation program is that mediation is a more effective process than court for resolving interpersonal disputes among urban dwellers who have on-going relationships. Traditionally, police and court personnel have been unable and increasingly unwilling to become involved in domestic disputes, lovers' quarrels, long-standing arguments between neighbors, and other kinds of personal or protracted arguments. Police say that are understaffed, overworked, and do not have the time necessary to talk through such complex disputes. Community mediation was designed to provide trained mediators for these types of interpersonal cases. Volunteers from the community were interviewed, screened, and intensively trained by a New York firm. Mediators are long-time residents of the community, and this enhances their ability to establish trust, rapport, and credibility with the complainants. In this sense, they substitute for community elders and family heads in the Middle Eastern setting. They have the community knowledge and experience necessary to understand each complainant's personal place in the community, they can place each case in a social context, and they understand the personal codes and references the complainants present during a mediation session.

THE MEDIATORS

At the core of the program is a group of people from the community who have been professionally trained as mediators. The mediators are a varied group in age, sex, race, background, occupation, and temperament.

For a few of the mediators this was their first experience in any kind of community work; the majority, however, had had varying degrees of community involvement in busing and desegregation efforts, housing, community redevelopment, foster child care, court work, and similar kinds of civic efforts.

The role and function of the mediators in relation to the complainants are synonymous with those we saw in the Middle East, but they have been successfully transferred to the urban American setting. The main points stressed throughout training are:

1. Mediators facilitate agreements between parties; they are not charged to decide if a legal rule has been broken or if one party is right and the other wrong.

2. Mediators must be very clear about this function and communicate it clearly to the parties and any witnesses at the beginning of a session.

3. Mediators must constantly work to develop their skills as trustworthy, impartial listeners. In a constant process of self-evaluation, mediators concur that their two most important skills are listening well and asking good questions. Good questions are those that elicit the desired information in a way that does not

irritate, offend, or intimidate a person, and the skills required to do so were evaluated by many participants as even more important than membership in the community. Community membership can help a mediator establish trust among the participants, but good mediation skills are essential to the success of a session and the strength of the agreement.

Mediators in this urban setting agree that age, more than sex or race, was a highly noticeable and sensitive variable in establishing rapport with disputants. When the complaining parties happened to be older than any of the panel members, the panel was referred to as "you kids," although two of the panel members were well into their 30s. Sex and race distributions within the mediation panels have not been difficult, but a conscious effort is made for each session to have a distribution according to age, sex, and race among the mediators.

4. Mediators should constantly focus on the problem and think ahead about possible resolutions, rather than worrying about controlling the immediate situation.

5. Mediators need training, experience, and a particular temperament to be able to gradually build the will to settle among the participants. It takes experience to judge, for example, when to keep the parties talking among themselves, and when to separate the parties, talk with them individually, and get to each person's final reason for resolution.

The training of community members teaches skills that generate the feelings of trust, empathy, and respect that characterize mediation in any social group. Residence in the community allows mediators and disputants to talk in terms of informal place names, particular streets, and common experiences; this knowledge of the community, its history, structure, and problems allows mediators to gradually establish rapport by drawing upon the commonality of shared experience. Although the networks of kinship, marriage, and alliance vary for each participant, trained community members serve in place of dense, face-to-face relationships. It is not that complainants' kin, allies, and friends do not become involved in the conflict, but for the duration of the mediation session(s), mediators fit into each person's specific, personal social networks in a meaningful and productive way.

THE MEDIATION PROCESS

The emphasis of mediation in any cultural setting is managing conflict, not punishing wrongdoers. Compensation or other kinds of restitution may be part of the final settlement, but that is not the primary function of the process. Reintegration of relationships, managing conflict, and relieving immediate overt disputes are the primary goals.

At the beginning of the mediation session, the mediators introduce themselves to both disputants. Disputants may bring witnesses or a lawyer for support, but

An Urban Mediation Program

this is both discouraged and actively controlled. Auxiliary people are quietly weeded out as mediation progresses. After introductions, everyone is seated at the same table, with the disputants at either end and the mediation panel in the middle. Ideally mediators work in groups of three, but sometimes only two mediators will handle a case.

After everyone is seated and comfortable, the person chairing the panel will begin by explaining the program, the function of mediation, how this particular mediation will proceed, and the role that the mediators will play. Each mediator speaks briefly during these introductory remarks in order to calm the tensions and familiarize the disputants with each of the mediators. Disputants are encouraged to be comfortable, smoke, take notes if they wish, and ask questions at any time. A mediator explains that the panel takes temporary notes throughout the session for their own use, but all notes are destroyed at the end of the session. The total confidentiality of the proceedings is made clear to both parties.

These preliminaries make it clear that this is not an adversary proceeding, and they—the disputants—are there to make the final resolution decisions, not the mediators. Everyone is seated at the same level, arms resting on the same table, and this symbolically sets a tone of equality; no participant is higher or lower than the other in this situation.

One mediator will then ask the complainant who sought the original complaint to begin by telling her or his story without interruption from the other party. After this version is recounted, the respondent has the same opportunity. Throughout the entire process, the mediators ask questions only for clarification and take notes on information they feel will be pertinent.

Rarely do these opening remarks proceed without interruption. Tempers and feelings are usually running high, and unless one person begins to dominate the conversation and storytelling, disputants are allowed to yell and argue with one another during this period.

At the end of both recitations, each disputant is asked to comment on the other's story, and if the preceding accounts went smoothly, it is at this point that the parties begin to argue and disagree with the versions and viewpoints that have been presented. Mediators encourage the disputants to talk, yell, and argue, and will interfere only if physical violence seems probable, or if the information becomes unproductively repetitive.

Mediators get a great deal of information from this type of free exchange between the disputants. True or hidden feelings, underlying causes, past relationships, the history of the dispute, other persons involved, parties' feelings about one another, and other information pours forth in rapid succession. Furthermore, this exchange gives the disputants a chance to ventilate anger and hostility in whatever form they choose, short of assault. There is no attempt to edit language style, profanity, gestures, or other forms of expression from the verbal exchange.

Next the panel begins *caucusing*, a term that is fully explained to the participants in the introductory remarks. Caucusing involves talking with each party separately, to let them talk freely without the other party present. Caucusing begins to explore the concrete outcomes each disputant would like to see from a settlement.

The mediators ask both parties to adjourn to separate rooms where they have coffee and comfortable chairs, then the mediators decide which disputant they will talk with first. Are someone's points still unclear? Is it clear that one party has more than one specific dispute on her or his mind? The mediators discuss such questions, their perceptions of the previous proceedings, and the information they have collected. They then must agree on what line of inquiry to pursue. They may be in agreement, or some mediators may have specific areas they would like to explore, while another mediator prefers to pursue a different set of questions.

Caucusing may be brief or extensive. It is critical that mediators agree on a questioning process, what points are still unclear, and precisely how they want to handle the individual discussions with either party. Clarification among themselves is crucial to smooth and cumulative efforts in dealing with the complainants.

As in the Middle Eastern setting, discussion proceeds back and forth with each party as often as necessary to clarify the facts and possible outcomes. Discussions with each disputant are very candid and open-ended. The disputant may again repeat the story of the dispute, add new facts, or tell the panel "how it really was" and "what the real beef is all about." Such open honesty is essential to getting at the underlying causes of the particular dispute. Each individual caucus session is confidential, and mediators ask at the end of each separate discussion if there is any information that the disputant does not want conveyed to the other party.

Caucusing continues until the mediators feel both parties have reached an agreement on all points. Even minor points are pursued with each party individually, because minor points that flare up at the point of resolution could sabotage a long process of agreement building on major issues. Finally, a settlement statement is outlined with each party, and only then are both disputants brought back together in the mediation room. This is identical to the Middle Eastern process in which disputants do not see one another directly until resolution is imminent.

In this final discussion minor points are solidified between the parties. The atmosphere is much calmer by this time, and the parties can sort out procedural or referral questions, read and evaluate the written agreement, and sign the agreement. The agreement is xeroxed immediately so each disputant has a copy to take home for personal reference. Mediation can last from 1 to 4 hours, and sometimes more than one session is required.

The power and the enforcement of the formal legal system remains behind the mediation settlement for 3 months during which the original complaint remains active and may be initiated at any time. If the mediation agreement is broken, any party may call the program and ask for another session. If this solution is not acceptable to either party, the original complaint goes into effect and there is a court hearing.

To illustrate these general principles in more specific detail and within a particular social context, Cases 11 and 12 are illustrative of cases mediated by the program. The cases are altered to protect the anonymity of the participants.

CASE 11. THE CASE OF THE STOLEN RING

Andrea H. has brought a complaint against George S. for breaking and entering, theft, and assault. Andrea is 26 years old, Black, a student, and a life-long resident of the community. George is 28 years old, Black, a carpenter, and lives in a nearby community. Both parties are single.

As Andrea began to tell her story, it became clear that she had known George for some time; they were friends. Andrea stated that she had not seen George for awhile, then one night when she returned home, she found him in her apartment going through the bureau drawers in her bedroom. She asked him what he was doing there and how he had gotten into the apartment.

When he admitted to having broken the latch on a back window to get inside, a terrible argument followed. The argument turned into a fight after he said he had come for a ring he had given her; he wanted it back. She started to yell and "beat on him to get out"; he hit her in the face and left. She said her face and jaw had been stiff and sore since the incident (3 days before) and that he was a common thief and ought to be punished.

George's version of the story was somewhat different. He said that not only were he and Andrea friends, but they had been engaged to be married. He had given her an engagement ring that had a diamond in it, and that was what he had been trying to get back. He said that he did not really break a latch to get in, but just gave it a good shove to force it open; it could be easily fixed, he said.

He then went into a 15-minute account of how Andrea had been unfaithful to him and had been going out with other guys after she had taken his ring. Then she refused to see him, he said, and would not give the ring back.

Andrea leaped up at this point to scream that she had never gone out with anybody else since he gave her the ring, that they had not made any definite plans, and that he did not own her every minute.

An argument erupted and gradually cooled down.

George finished his version of the dispute by explaining how he had gotten into the apartment, how he had been very careful not to bother anything, and just went looking for the ring. He had figured it would not be hard to find. He further said that he had come over to ask Andrea for the ring, but when he had found that she was not at home, he had decided to take things into his own hands and get the ring himself. He knew this was wrong, he said, but he was angry and upset and did not think anybody would get hurt.

Then another argument started up between the parties about why he had hit her in the first place—she had been astounded at that because he had always been nice, and he said he had also surprised himself. Finally the arguing lost steam, and both parties agreed that they had finished their version of the dispute.

During caucusing, which began with Andrea, the story developed in detail. Andrea said she had been visiting old high-school friends with one of the men from her class and that George had seen them, but she did not count that as a date or cheating or being unfaithful. George had not given her a chance to explain this, and that had made her mad, so she refused to talk to him when he called repeatedly on the phone. Andrea gradually decided that she really wanted to forget the whole thing and sit down and talk to George.

George had calmed down by the time he met with the mediators for caucusing. He was sorry he had broken in and frightened her. One of the mediators told George that Andrea had mentioned being frightened at seeing him there, especially when she had not known who it was. The mediator asked George if he had considered that when he broke in. George said he had not, and was ready to accept the fact that she hit him and yelled at him because she had been badly frightened.

Both parties were talked with individually two times, and it was clear at the end of that time that Andrea wanted to make up, and George wanted to make up and wanted her to keep the ring.

The two parties were brought back together, and they talked for 30 to 45 minutes about what had happened, how they felt, and why they had not been able to talk to one another. Andrea explained about the high-school friends and George admitted he had been hurt and jealous and had flown off the handle.

The final agreement in this case stated that Andrea agreed to drop the charges against George, and George agreed to give her back the ring and to continue their relationship, but never to break into her apartment, no matter what the circumstances.

This case ended happily. The agreement held for 3 months, and Andrea and George stayed together and set a date for the wedding. Although the consequences of this case are not as violent or substantive as some other cases, the charges against George were serious ones and could have caused him serious trouble if he had gone before a judge. Although this case ultimately needed a couple counselor, that need was embedded in a legal dispute and complaint that

An Urban Mediation Program

needed airing and understanding before progress could be made on the interpersonal issue.

Assault and battery cases between husbands and wives account for a large proportion of the family disputes (67%). All of these cases are initiated by women, indicating that the women in this community need forums other than the courts in which to seek assistance with problems of abuse, neglect, and harassment. By their own accounts, women feel that the mediation program gives them a place to bring problems they had often thought were hopeless.

Case 12 is a case brought by one such woman; it is a case involving long-term frustration, abuse, and isolation. It is one of those difficult cases where mediators, and perhaps even the disputing parties, know that the final agreement will probably break down. All parties to this dispute agree, however, that considerable progress of a personal and social nature had been made as this first agreement was reached. The woman in the case, Marian, was especially vocal in her relief that she had found a safe forum where she could air and possibly begin to resolve this domestic problem.

CASE 12. A BATTERED WIFE

Marian C. is 36 years old, white, Irish, and Catholic. She has brought a complaint against her husband, Paul C., for assault. The couple has six children, ages 17, 16, 13, 12, 9, 6. Marian works part time as a sales clerk during the day. Paul is 42 years old, white, Irish, and Catholic also. He is a longshoreman and often works night shifts as well as days. Both were born and raised in the community.

During the preliminary discussion the assault was discussed. Paul returned home one Saturday afternoon with two friends; they brought five or six cases of beer with them. Soon two other men arrived at the door. The men gathered in the kitchen; it was the end of a long 16-day work stretch for them and they had 4 days off and planned to celebrate. They proceeded to drink, tell stories, and talk about union business.

Marian fixed them some dinner when she prepared food for herself and the four younger children. Other than that she left them alone. "When he gets like this there isn't any way I want to be around him." Marian had planned to go to her sister's that evening because she had a new baby and Marian had not seen her in several weeks. At 4:00 P.M. this had been fine with Paul; he would have the house to himself. At 9:00 P.M. this was not fine with Paul because he did not want to be left with the four kids in case he and the guys wanted to go out. The two older children were out.

Marian left and went to her sister's house after the kids were settled for the night. She got back around midnight. Paul's friends had left and he was very drunk. She had hoped he would be asleep in the bedroom or on the couch, but he was in the kitchen. A heated argument ensued.

Paul called her worthless, a tramp, a whore, and a host of other names. She let these go by, she said, because "he really doesn't mean them and usually says he's sorry in a day or two." Paul began to hit her with his fists and to slap her around the kitchen; then he picked up a wooden kitchen chair and threw it at her. Part of the chair caught on her lip and cut deep into her cheek and face. Marian ran from the room after that scene, but Paul remained in the kitchen shouting and screaming. Marian left the house and went back to her sister's, taking the younger children and leaving a note for the older two that she would be back the next morning.

Paul did not deny any of this version of the story. He said he had lost his head, gotten angry, and hit her; he did not remember the details of hitting her. He was sorry.

Private caucusing with each party individually revealed other problems and tensions. This was not an isolated incident. This was not the first time she had been physically assaulted; for nearly 10 years Paul had consistently beaten her when he was drunk: "When he comes home drunk, or comes home and gets drunk then he beats on me. Well that's it. I've had enough. It's not good for my kids, it's not good for me. I don't want a divorce. He's a good man otherwise, but I can't stand him to hit me again."

In exploring what Marian really wanted out of a settlement, it turned out there were other things. She wanted to be able to go out once in a while to see her family, and she wanted occasionally to go out to dinner or the movies. In the last 5 years, she said, all Paul ever offered as a night out was to go out to the hockey game in town.

Paul said that Marian used to respect him and be a good wife, but now he felt she did not really notice him much or care about him. She spent most of her time at home with the kids. He was under a lot of pressure on the job; there were some tensions there, and some problems in the union, and he constantly worried about layoffs. He spent a lot of time talking about his work. "Hey, you know, everybody belts somebody sometime. All the guys do. I don't usually mean it. I love her. But sometimes she just drives me nuts."

[Note: As some various sources of agreement began to emerge, one of the major obstacles for resolving these disputes became evident as well. Mediators are strictly trained not to impose their views on the disputing parties but to help them reach their own agreement. This raises the question for mediators "of how far you go to convince somebody that they may have a drinking problem. A guy drinks a case of beer in a night, then beats on his wife, but he doesn't think he's an alcoholic. He thinks lots of guys drink that much (personal interview)."]

In this case, the mediators gently pressed on Paul to see how open he was to getting help to deal with his drinking and violence. He was not willing to seek help for those issues, but he was willing to get some marital counseling because his wife was asking for it and because he admitted there were problems. He felt that the real problem was that communication between him and his wife had totally broken down.

For Marian, this was the first time in over 10 years that she felt she had actually done something about her life and her marriage. She openly stated during private discussions that she loved her husband, but she had often thought of just taking the kids and leaving him while he was at work; she felt that she could not realistically afford to do that. Her sister's advice had finally sent her to court to file a formal complaint. Marian had worried that this might make Paul angrier than he already was, but she had decided to go through with it, she said, "because I'd just run out of things to do. I'd tried lots of times and nothing worked."

Marian and Paul reached an agreement in which Marian agreed not to bring up the past, to try to establish some trust in Paul, and to try to understand Paul's work schedule and problems. Paul agreed to meet friends outside the house, talk about problems, let Marian see her family when she wished, stop all physical abuse, use a counselor, and take his wife out once a week outside the community.

This agreement broke down after 6 weeks, but the couple called the program office and asked to schedule another session. Another session was held; the mediators were able to make more progress toward Paul's accepting a referral to a local agency to talk about his drinking. The mediators knew that the first agreement was weak and that the next time Paul drank the old patterns would repeat themselves. The first agreement actually held up through several drinking episodes, but when the verbal and physical abuse resumed, the couple knew they needed help.

Marian and Paul's agreement is a relatively typical one; some are more general, while others are more specific in details, depending on the style of the two parties. All agreements are very case-specific and deal with the disputant's particular needs. While the original agreement had a central weakness in that it did not directly deal with the drinking problem, it had set in motion a discussion and participation pattern for Marian that allowed the couple, and particularly Marian, to begin to deal with their problems.

OUTCOMES

A number of mediators expressed feelings of doubt and nervous anticipation which they experienced after the training session and before actual mediation began. "It was hard for me to believe that we could really create a situation where people would talk about their personal problems [personal interview]." Such anxieties are common among new mediators and are gradually worked out in practice. The mediators agreed that after the first case in which they all feared that they would make a fatal mistake, they developed a personal style and accommodated to the styles of others.

Collectively, the first training group of mediators evaluated the program after 8 months of experience. Their analysis is compiled from lengthy interviews with each mediator at the end of the program's first year. The arguments and variables are presented as close to the way the mediators described them as possible.

First, mediators noted that the mediation session is often the first time that disputants have the opportunity to actually sit and listen to the other person's side of the story. In a court hearing the parties usually do not speak at all. Thus, complainants never hear the other's perceptions of the dispute, or the effects of that dispute on individuals' lives.

Second, mediators unanimously commented on the atmosphere of trust established in the mediation session. Once confidence and trust has been developed in the panel, as one mediator remarked, "the real problems start to surface." Once people know they *can* discuss everything that is on their minds that *they feel* is related to the conflict, they start to deal with underlying issues in what is often a prolonged conflict. Mediators noted that it was common to hear "you know, this is the first time I really understood the problem from her or his point of view" from disputants after a case has been settled.

Third, people can talk to each other. Since it is the role of the mediators to facilitate an agreement that the parties themselves create, the interaction between the parties is vital in working toward a shared understanding. In court, mediators and disputants say, the clerk or judge often "talks at" the people involved, but rarely will the parties be allowed to talk with one another. The court's task of finding a guilty party precludes free interaction. Mediators strongly agreed that it is very important for people to talk in a manner that has meaning for them. Disputants use slang, present beliefs and values that are culturally relevant to them, and discuss the circumstances of their personal lives.

Fourth, mediators noted that people feel they are actively participating in the process of solving their own problems. There are no bureaucracies to wait for and depend on, no people telling you what you should do, and no administrative time delays to work your life and job around. Although there is a link to the court through the original complaint, the process is different. The feeling of helplessness and being "done unto" in the court system is eliminated; people do for themselves in mediating conflict.

For the mediators themselves, the characteristics of the mediation process combine to give them a knowledge that they are facilitating problem solving, contrary to much of their previous community work which involved constant haggling with bureaucracies or landlords with minimal results. Furthermore, the participants themselves have been outspoken, enthusiastic, and sometimes emotional in their evaluation of the mediation process. Many who have spoken to the mediators or the staff state emphatically that they wish the program had existed for them much sooner.

Urban Mediation Case Materials

Although the program originated with a focus on referrals from the clerk, figures for the first 2 years show that the primary sources of referrals are judges, followed by the clerk, self-referral, and the police (Table 7.1).

The "self" category involves various types of personal referral. Referrals from participants or other community members are typical of this category, but some people have taken the individual initiative to walk into the office from the street and ask if the program can help them with a problem.

Of this total number of cases, family disputes have been referred with the highest frequency, followed by disputes between neighbors and friends. A more complete breakdown is given in Table 7.2.

Of the total number of cases referred to the program in a 2-year period (611), 181 (30%) withdrew. This number includes disputants who simply did not want to mediate, but preferred to press charges in the district court, as well as cases that were inappropriately referred to the program.

During the first 2 years the mediation program held 412 mediation sessions. Of this total number of completed sessions, 302 cases (73%) were settled, 53 cases were not settled (13%), and 57 cases (14%) broke down after mediation had been completed.

A more detailed breakdown of the types of cases referred will provide a clearer statistical picture of where the strengths of the program have been most evident (Table 7.3).

The 214 cases involving family disputes constitute 35% of the total referred cases. Of these cases, 72% were successfully mediated, while 26% of them withdrew, and 2% were still in progress at the time of the analysis. There was one direct social service referral from this group of cases.

TABLE 7.1
Mediation Program—Referrals Received
(November 1975 to November 1977)[a]

Referral source	Percentage of total
Bench	58
Clerk	32
Self	8
Police	2
	100%

[a]N = 611 cases.

TABLE 7.2
Mediation Program—Types of Referred Cases
(November 1975 to November 1977)[a]

Type of case	Percentage of total
Family	35
Neighbors	22
Friends	18
Other	13
Landlord/tenant	10
Merchant/consumer	1
School	1
	100%

[a] N = 611.

Disputes between neighbors (136) comprised 22% of the total referrals; 67% of these cases were mediated, while 30% withdrew, and 3% were in progress.

Disputes between friends (109) comprised 18% of all the cases; 67% of these were mediated, 28% withdrew, and 5% were in progress.

Disputes between individuals who were strangers at the time of conflict (81) made up 13% of the total referrals; 62% of these cases were mediated, 35% withdrew, and 3% were in progress.

Only 9% of all the cases (55) involved landlords and tenants; 60% of these were mediated; 38% withdrew, and 2% were still in progress. Another small sampling—merchant and consumer complaints (9)—made up only 2% of all referrals, but the success rate was high; 78% of these disputes were mediated and 22% withdrew.

The final sampling involved school personnel, parents, or students in conflict. While this category only contained 7 cases or 1% of the total referrals, 5 of these cases were successfully mediated and only 2 cases withdrew.

The 2-year case materials show that the program deals effectively with cases that proceed to mediation. A mediation success rate of nearly 75% is a very encouraging sign of success.

Mediation works in this urban setting. There is no type of case in which the success rate falls below 60%, and most are considerably higher. The 60% success category—landlord–tenant disputes—also represents a category in which clear-cut financial considerations (either payments or repairs) are the focus of the disagreement. The Middle Eastern cases illustrated that even in a society where mediation is a long-established tradition, there is an increasing tendency to formalize or adjudicate cases involving straight financial gain or loss.

TABLE 7.3
Mediation Program—Breakdown of Case Referrals (November 1975 to November 1977)[a]

	Family	Neighbors	Friends	Other	Landlord/tenant	Merchant/consumer	School
Percentage mediated	72	67	67	62	60	78	71
Percentage withdrew	26	30	28	35	38	22	29
Percentage in progress	2	3	5	3	2	—	—
Total percentage	100	100	100	100	100	100	100
Number of cases	214	136	109	81	55	9	7

[a] $N = 611$ cases.

The program maintains this success rate even in the midst of a case load that includes felonies and misdemeanors. Other experimental programs usually do not include such difficult and time-consuming cases, but often tend to prefer technical, high-turnover cases such as bad checks, consumer fraud, and shoplifting. Thus, although this mediation program operates at a higher comparative cost per case than other programs, the difficulty of the cases offsets this cost–benefit differential.

Cost figures can further be misleading by dealing with the number of cases rather than the number of individuals involved. Calculations based on at least two disputants for each case better demonstrate the overall cost effectiveness of the program. Such calculations reveal that the cost per client in the mediation program is about $145. Thus, although the unit cost per client is relatively high, the program staff does not feel that this is an unreasonable amount, especially in the light of rising court costs, the number of people served, and the serious nature of the types of cases accepted. While the program could increase its case load and lower its per-client costs, the staff and supporters in the court feel that the absolute cost is not extremely high and that the quality of the service is extremely sound.

Program costs have also been reduced over the initial 2-year period. The recent U.S. LEAA (1978) review of the program summarized the case costs, which are still higher than other similar pilot projects, as products of two main factors:

> (1) The model of community involvement necessarily involves higher administrative costs due to the need for tighter management controls, more extensive training and recruitment, and more time to develop and sustain community interest.
>
> (2) The project operates under a multilevel administrative structure. As one component of a larger program effort... the mediation project shares central project management expenses, incurs some administrative expenses for its parent organization, and is assessed a substantial amount for city overhead expense [p. 107].

The training of mediators is a continuing strength of the program. The training function is handled internally by program mediators, so that reliance on an outside training agency is no longer necessary. This also makes the training more locally specific, and trainers can focus on the particular types of cases that are current and typical of the community.

While it is true that individual's life-styles are complex and varied, the use of a heterogeneous group of mediators familiar with the community integrates this diversity quite well. The mixture and balance in terms of race, sex, age, and backgrounds has proved an invaluable tool not only for mediating disputes, but for strengthening ties and understanding between people in the community as well.

The mediation program demonstrates the greatest success in cases where the people have an on-going interpersonal relationship, and where friction has developed around one or two key issues. The less successful types of cases that pass through the program are the victims of shoplifting, bad checks, consumer fraud, and similar kinds of phenomena where the perpetrator is unknown or extremely powerful. It has been possible to mediate conflict involving an entire neighborhood, but is very hard if neighborhood people have only a short history of interaction with one another. Program administrators feel that successful mediation in an urban setting depends on a willingness to mediate, the threat of an activated complaint if mediation fails, the community relationships that provide a basis for finding shared understandings, and building toward future interests. An interpersonal relationship is not the sole prerequisite for successful mediation in this setting, but the success rate is clearly higher when this type of relationship exists between disputing parties.

Conclusions

The success of mediation in this program is a quantitatively measurable fact. The principles of mediation have been successfully implemented—first in the training of the mediators and secondly in the participants. The introductory discussion between participants and mediators sets the stage for the subsequent operationalization of the principles during the actual mediation. Most participants voluntarily choose mediation because they wish a private settlement that the other party will adhere to, and because they do not necessarily want to punish the other party. Participants have an on-going or important relationship with the other disputant within the same community, they are willing to express personal concerns and needs in relation to a conciliatory outcome, they believe the process is fair and egalitarian, and they have pride and satisfaction at stake, as well as tangible resources.

People dealing with people often do not want to raise a dispute to the level of public reprisal; we have seen illustrations of this from two cultures. Parties mediating a dispute are more interested in resolving the conflict and restoring some kind of workable equilibrium than in assigning guilt in win-or-lose terms. Such cases are easily removed from the criminal and civil adjudicatory process with great savings in terms of court time, management, and expense. The personal benefits that the participants can potentially derive from mediation are clearly valuable outcomes.

Although it was noted that an on-going interpersonal relationship was not the sole criteria for successful mediation within the program, this variable has emerged as one of the most consistent indicators of probable success. The program administration theorized that this would be the case, so during the initial year of operation limited cases to those involving some degree of viable, on-going social relationship. This strategy allowed mediators to learn their skills with cases that indicated a high probability of success, and bolstered the program's initial year with demonstrable success figures.

Limiting cases in this way also tended to initially constrain the types of resources at the base of interpersonal conflict. Although the program deals successfully with disputes over tangible and intangible resources, the high incidence of interpersonal cases allows more personal issues such as fears, anger, guilt, stress, and helplessness to be dealt with during the resolution of the conflict.

Personal stress and a sense of powerlessness to do anything to relieve that stress were constant themes in mediators' and informants' statements. Personal stress was often months or years in duration, and people exhibited mild to severe forms of physical, psychosomatic, and mental health symptoms as a result. Some participants were aware of these symptoms and mentioned them to mediators during or after the session, and other symptoms were noted by the mediators and discussed in interviews after the first year.

Symptoms of stress that were noted in association with tension and protracted conflict among disputants were allergies, migraine headaches, asthma, rashes, high blood pressure, alcoholism, and fatigue. Although such symptoms are frequently treated as medical problems needing medical attention, they are also recognized as psychological reactions to stress which respond to therapeutic interventions, including ventilation of feelings, resolution, or progress toward resolution of a conflict (Muench, 1963; O'Connor, 1977). Mediation provides a mechanism by which disputants can act and interact within the context of their own lives toward solving interpersonal conflicts. O'Connor (1977) has noted that psychosomatic patients who traditionally are willing to accept only medical treatment, accept therapeutic intervention when it is offered in a medical setting. Similarly, disputants in the mediation program accept therapeutic and counseling services when offered as a part of dispute resolution.

Among the disputing parties in the mediation program, people stated that they felt powerless to effect "the system." Allowing individuals as much time as they deem necessary to portray their conflict situation in their own terms in an atmosphere of empathy and trust is not only therapeutic, but participants say it greatly diminishes feelings of powerlessness and the isolating effects of urban living.

Disputants do not always have a clear idea of what they want or how they really feel in a given situation. It takes time and the proper environment to find out. Mediators are trained to pick up cues in the uncensored conversation and argument, piece together the elements on which the two parties agree, and in some cases act as gentle agents of reality when one party rerefuses to acknowledge the other party's feelings or point of view.

In the courtroom, expression and discussion is constrained by the propriety and authority structured into the setting. In mediation, regardless of the degree of shared community identity, participants are given a forum to define their problem and their community in a personally relevant way.

A dissatisfaction with and a disconnection from the law and the court system makes community mediation a workable alternative for many of the program participants. This cultural and political distance from the law was quite pronounced, particularly among women complainants. Participants and mediators consistently reported that disputants feel, in varying degrees, that the court "doesn't work for them" and is too dangerous, expensive, and complicated.

The mediation process in this urban program fosters equality and egalitarianism between disputants in every phase. From the equality of treatment to the distribution of participants in physical space, the conciliatory goal lessens tensions initially created by power or status inequalities. Satisfaction with the outcome by both parties is not sacrificed to the egalitarian ideal, however.

Middle Eastern family and network sanctions are replaced by the formal sanction of the court in the American setting. The threat of an active complaint that can be revived if mediation is uncompleted or subsequently fails is an important equalizing factor. It is the element of power needed to curb tempers, equalize relationships of unequal power and/or prestige, and add legitimacy to the proceedings. Mediation does not rest entirely on the good will of disputing parties, and it does not sacrifice the needs of a weaker party; it works with deterrents and potential sanctioning power to make parties think about the consequences of refusing to negotiate a settlement. This threat of force is an essential element in seeing that parties to a dispute, particularly the respondents, take the program and the mediation process seriously and realistically. This threat is coercive in a mild sense, but without the strong social control of the community, it is necessary. The threat of formal sanction is not coercive in a strong sense, however, because mediation is voluntary.

One final aspect of the program is that it eliminates some of the hidden costs of court proceedings and is, therefore, much fairer to low- or fixed-income individuals.

It is easier for an individual making $15,000 working in a front office to get the morning off to go frequently to court than it is for an individual making $5,000 in the back room of the same office to do the same. Court appearances also require expenditures for transportation, child care, and food during the hours of waiting.

The mediation program is able to schedule sessions at the disputants' convenience, so people do not lose valuable work time in trying to resolve a personal conflict. Sessions are held during the day, but more frequently in the evenings and on weekends. Since the program is community based, transportation has not been a serious problem; coffee is provided free of charge.

The implementation of the principles of mediation and administrative awareness of the social variables that must be present or altered to insure successful mediation have created a community mediation program that works. While the same distance from the formal legal system encourages renewal and survival of local community mechanisms in both the Lebanese and American cases, the urban American setting substitutes formal complaints for community and family social control; lack of systematic alternatives for homogeneous, shared community values; and neighborhood identity for family identity. Both settings use the threat of police and court involvement as an important equalizer and catalyst for local resolutions.

The American community mediation program not only exhibits quantifiable success and cost figures that are favorable or superior to lawyer and court-related costs, but it demonstrates, through disputants' and mediators' own testimony, that the personal gains from mediation are far-ranging and pervasive, as well as uniquely individual.

8
Conclusions

The two comparative case studies illustrate the theoretical propositions of the theory of mediation, and provide a cross-cultural comparison of working mediation systems. The Lebanese mediation case material has direct relevance to questions of legal organization and change in the United States, particularly those issues related to the recent debates over the viability of community mediation (Danzig and Lowy, 1975; Felstiner, 1974, 1975), and reorganization of the lower court system (Mayhew and Reiss, 1969; Packer, 1968; Danzig, 1973; Galanter, 1975, 1976; Marks, 1976; Mayhew, 1975; Rabin, 1976; Sarat, 1976, 1977).

In America, courts are a central figure in discussions of dispute settlement. Discontent with the lower court system was detailed early in the century by Roscoe Pound (1906). The American court system has evolved since that time from the informal, time-consuming administration of justice to the more efficient bureaucratic forms of judicial administration (Witty, 1970). Courts, particularly at the district and municipal levels, are plagued with continuations, clogged dockets, inaccurate record keeping, voluminous paperwork, and administrative inefficiency.

The anonymous and fragmented environment of our urban communities is often thought to preclude any real citizen participation in court or community programs. Therefore, many scholars argue that change in the lower courts should focus on the revision of codes, conflicts in jurisdictions, efficiency of operation, and consistency of functioning.

Like Lebanon, the United States is a plural society that has been succinctly defined by Furnival in Barth (1969) as a

> poly-ethnic society integrated in the market place, under the control of a state system dominated by one of the groups, but leaving large areas of cultural diversity in the religious and domestic sectors of activity [p. 16].

The United States has a great deal in common with Lebanon regardless of the difference in size between the two countries (See Benedict, 1962, 1965, 1968; Hudson, 1968; Morris, 1967; Kuper and Smith, 1971). Galanter (1976) notes strong parallels between the transition from the administration of justice to judicial administration that the United States has experienced, and the shift from traditional to modern types of legal procedures that Lebanon is experiencing. Addressing such transitions comparatively, as the two case studies have done, must include observations on the power of individuals to make choices about their lives and their conflicts, and the power involved in defining and implementing appropriate dispute resolution.

In American society, one can ignore, exit from, and avoid many types of interpersonal conflict (Felstiner, 1974; Hirshman, 1970). In the Middle Eastern community, avoidance is possible through structured "nontalking" relationships between persons and families, but it is very infrequent. People in Shehaam are not anonymous in any social sense, and their choice to avoid comes after activation of various alternative systems available to ameriliorate conflict. In contrast, the absence of systematic alternative processes to resolve conflict in the United States can lead to constant repression, which generates feelings of frustration and powerlessness on the part of individual citizens (Auerback, 1976; Galanter, 1974; Lerner, 1976; Nader and Singer, 1976; Spradley, 1973).

This comparison of mediation in two social settings demonstrates that American urban communities and traditional communities are not examples of total contrast. Part of the current debate over appropriate processes of conflict management in the United States minimizes the similarities among communities both local and cross-cultural. Felstiner (1974) argues that in modern, technical societies "adjudication and mediation of disputes will be hard to institutionalize and avoidance will carry significantly lower costs [p. 82]." He goes on to say:

> Institutionalzed mediation of interpersonal disputes will also be infrequent in a TCRS (technologically complex, rich society)... where role differentiation is intense, few persons are qualified by experience to mediate any disputes: everybody's role set is too specialized to be common experience with a significant number of potential disputants... [p. 83].

This argument seriously underestimates the personal and mental health costs to individuals from the lack of responsive remedy agents for continually unresolved stress, competition, and conflict (Danzig and Lowy, 1975).

8. Conclusions

The Middle Eastern data show that although Lebanese villagers are less specialized than Americans in role sets, they share a common experience and identity with a local, self-defined group. Many Americans share that community identity whether it is based on ethnicity, race, occupation, or length of residence. Tensions in the two cultures are from different sources and are woven into a different cultural pattern, but the struggle for political and economic survival is a reality in both settings.

It is clear that most Americans live with (a) varying degrees of stress and conflict, (b) some working definition of what their neighborhood or community is, (c) neighborhood conflict—both internal and external, and (d) interpersonal conflict with family members and outsiders (Hannerz, 1969; Kornblum, 1974; Stack, 1974; Suttles, 1968; Rubin, 1976; Warner, 1959; for examples from England, see also Young and Willmott, 1957; Byles and Morris, 1977).

The data also show that Middle Eastern villagers know one another in an intensive, personal way, but the cases illustrated that personal interaction is not the only factor that influences their ability to mediate and intermediate conflict. Shared values, distrust, and a lack of understanding about the court system; a sense of local community; personal support networks; the personal satisfaction of ventilating grievances; the involvement of local elites; the desire to settle outside formal structures; and, periodic community flare-ups that need dampening are all strong complementary reasons why mediation works continuously and effectively in Lebanon.

The Middle Eastern mediation process grows out of the villagers' self-perceived and self-defined needs for efficient conflict management. The theory of mediation posits that mediation in any society grows out of individuals' awareness of their community and their position in it. Mediation also continually deals with causes of conflict while legal systems have a tendency to deal with symptoms of conflict in the form of broken rules.

Sarat (1977) in a review of public opinion studies related to courts, notes that "Courts are not particularly visible or salient to the American people. The level of public awareness and knowledge of courts, court personnel, and court decisions is quite low [p. 438]." Even courts that were ostensibly organized to give citizens a local forum to redress personal grievances became forums for business, local government, and utility companies to pursue and litigate against individual citizens (Yngvesson and Hennessy, 1975). Such examples are comparable to the court system in Lebanon which reaches into the villages to pursue state and commercial business against individual villagers.

In the United States, individuals have few places to turn in times of conflict other than to the courts. Unlike Lebanon, communities and courts are directly linked to one another in the United States because there are no other mechanisms *systematically* available to individuals or communities. Certainly people can avoid or take matters into their own hands (self-help such as action lines, small claims court, direct negotiation), but such action has only recently proven positive, appropriate, and productive.

In the Middle East, personal anonymity is not a characteristic of community organization, but the disparity between the legal principles of users and practitioners is similar. A conceptual gap exists in both Lebanon and the United States between (*a*) the abstract, internal development of legal concepts at the top, through professionalization and case law that focuses primarily on legal concepts, and (*b*) individual needs for redress, justice, and satisfaction that grow out of life experience—community and cultural background.

Formal and informal conflict management systems exist or are created with two complementary but separate goals. The theory of mediation hypothesizes that one system exists or is created in response to the other. If their functions are overlapping (they want to resolve disputes) but diametrically opposed (they do so from distinctly different value systems), then cultural distance, social stratification, and community solidarity will determine the degree to which informal mechanisms remain viable. If the pervasive, informal function is to redress interpersonal disputes and the formal function is to generate a system of legal standards and philosophical concepts, then at least two systems of dispute settlement can coexist within one polity.

Several systems of legitimate dispute resolution operating with legitimacy within the same polity could be viewed as a social and legal asset, rather than as a political liability. The efforts of scholars and planners to draw everyone in a plural social system into a monolithic legal system must be systematically reevaluated. The so-called problems of legal pluralism could be viewed as assets if legal pluralism and its consequences were analyzed at various social and legal levels. A resolution of village, regional, and national needs may well require the integration of mediation, intermediation, and adjudication into one national integrated policy of conflict management. Mere access to legal services within the formal legal system is not enough.

Magavern, Thomas, and Stuart (1975) have argued that, particularly for the urban poor, the service approach to dispute settlement is misdirected. The service approach aims to provide the user with improved rights and benefits through existing legal institutions; the assumption is that only the delivery mechanisms are ineffective, and improvement will bring satisfaction (see Cahn and Cahn, 1966). This approach belongs to the "trickle down" philosophy of social policy and change that presumes that when conditions are improved for the elite economic sector, societal conditions will automatically improve as resources trickle downward and improve general living conditions.

If the American urban poor—or as the Lebanese case illustrates, the rural agricultural populations—have no actively enforceable power or influence within the existing legal structure, their increased participation in that system will continue to be as defendants and victims, not as active users. Without the

8. Conclusions

appropriate political and legal institutions to generate policies favorable to all segments of diverse populations, people will resist or withdraw from the formal arena, and struggle to keep their local conflict managing mechanisms strong and free from outside control. In Huntington's terms (1968), this kind of dialectical struggle amounts to political decay rather than political development. Magavern et al. (1975) echo this sentiment when they note that "as modernization mobilizes new social forces without a corresponding development of political institutions, traditional systems of authority are impaired, but not replaced, by effective new systems [p. 105]."

The solution to this development problem requires reorganizing priorities to open a restructured legal system to all economic groups, and to plan for the input of those groups into the formation of such a system. There are many different views and interpretations of legal needs. As this analysis shows, multiple conflict management systems often establish separate procedures that operate in opposition to one another, with neither aware of the strengths and advantages of the other.

Input from the local level must increase in the planning process—in America and elsewhere—and goals of administrators and planners must be reshaped as well. It is planners, administrators, and community advocates who can implement new legal institutions and policies to be more effective for all segments of a population.

It is often assumed that developing nations need only proper guidance, rules, and incentive to emerge with modern, adapted versions of western legal systems. Since western countries have had longer to sift through solutions to problems of jurisdiction, pleadings and procedures, international commercial and monetary codes, and legislation, it is believed that nations seeking development in the legal sphere only need to adopt western statutes and codes to eliminate problems in these areas. The case studies presented here challenge the effectiveness of such an ideology for planning a legal system that serves all sectors of a diverse population equally.

Rural participation in planned and unplanned change has been recognized as an essential ingredient in smooth social transitions (Eisenstadt, 1965; Roos and Roos, 1971). Studies within this framework have taken various forms. Huntington (1968) and others (see Bailey, 1969; Frey, 1965; Harris, 1968; Lerner and Gorden, 1969; Rustow, 1966; Quandt, 1970) have investigated the changing character of urban political elites and increased rural participation in change programs using concepts such as "ruralizing elections" and "want–get" ratios. These methods measure quantifiable degrees of change in specific variables after implementation.

Others, such as Katz (1965), Puchala (1968), and Hass (1971) have stressed social learning, bargaining, and redefining interessts in understanding and predicting when people will change behavior patterns and what kinds of pressure it takes to get them to do so. Throughout these kinds of studies there is little connection between quantifiable measures of change and the local peoples' perception of the changing situation. There is also an implicit assumption that individuals want access to the new system as it exists.

But access to progress and its concomitant programs is not the simple solution. As Befu (1967) and others have noted, the movement and reality of encroaching authority structures for rural, traditional populations seems irrevocable. If, as Haas (1971) describes, this irrevocable process of regional integration and national development "assumes the identity of political postulates concerning common purpose and common need among actors irrespective of level of action, [p. 19]" it will ignore the strength and importance of local-level politics, regional integration as locally perceived, traditional ideology, and pluralism (Frank, 1968; Friedrich, 1968).

The real effect of political elites, village leaders, regional and national administrators, support networks, and mediational processes must become more integrated in long-range social and legal planning. Given the pervasive traditional values and interlocking support and control networks outlined in the Lebanese material, it is clear that it is also necessary to understand community social organization in order to divert local and national interests from a collision course.

Implementing community mediation programs requires long-range planning. The principles of mediation must be fully understood, the propositions must be skillfully turned into administrative procedures, and in-take training and review procedures must mesh a particular community's needs with the effective provision of locally generated services. Cahn and Cahn (1966), long-standing proponents of legal services at the neighborhood level, also note that extensive, locally generated alternatives to the legal system must remain procedurally free from the dominance of that system.

> In effect, the legal system exercises a monopoly on what constitutes a grievance. . . . So long as this monopoly continues, so long as it is free to define for itself to what demands it must listen, and on what terms, and what remedies are appropriate, then the bulk of grievances and needs will never receive a full or fair hearing—or rational and full exposition [p. 41].

The input and response of users of the legal apparatus and its alternatives is critically important to implementing systematic, responsive flexibility in the legal system; such input must not be bound within the legal profession (see Cahn and Cahn, 1964, 1966, 1970; Auerbach, 1976; Cramton, 1975; Handler, Hollingsworth, and Erlanger, 1978). People must become aware of the range of options that can be open to them as a neighborhood or a community. Community people also need to begin discussing the benefits of mediation and courts in the context of their own communities. Then, people need to develop the knowl-

8. Conclusions

edge and skill to begin to implement real change into the local legal apparatus. What each community sees as the limitations of the courts and the potential benefits of creating mediational alternatives will undoubtedly be different. Such differences will work toward the effective functioning of the mediation process in each community; however, legal and mediational needs must be locally self-defined. Administratively the programs must understand the principles and functions of the mediation process and create a responsive, effective implementation plan, but the range or types of cases that come voluntarily to a mediation program can be ultimately left to the community itself.

While it is true that law is a reflection of values of some segment of a society, there is always a time lag between formal rules, rule changes, and customary behavior. In a plural society such as the United States, this time lag is further exacerbated by ethnic, religious, and racial differences. Mediation programs insert self-defined legal and social needs into the system of resolving interpersonal disputes and create some continuity between local communities and larger bureaucratic institutions. The urban mediation program profiled in Chapter 7 has clearly generaged interest, relief, and activity in segments of the community. The increasing number of walk-in self-referrals indicates that the benefits of the program are gradually spreading throughout the community.

The importance of self-defined groups is contained in Barth's (1969) discussion of groups and social boundaries:

> The critical focus... becomes the ethnic boundary that defines the group, not the cultural stuff that it encloses. The boundaries to which we must give our attention are of course social boundaries, though they may have territorial counterparts. If a group maintains its identity when members interact with others, this entails criteria for determining membership and ways of singnaling membership and exclusion... [p. 15].

Barth demonstrates that an in-group definition and the social process of boundary maintenance are healthy and necessary aspects of social organization and personal identity. By allowing groups and neighborhoods to self-define their boundaries and interests, community mediation programs provide legitimacy and valuable services to community groups.

Systematic implementation of mediation programs ultimately rests with the community and effective program administration, but part of the change and creativity will, hopefully, also come from within the legal profession.

By recognizing the limits of adjudication in certain types of cases, lawyers and judges could give important political impetus to mediation programs in their local jurisdictions. Such support must be encouraged and organized within the legal profession as an adjunct advocacy function of mediation program administrators, social policy planners, and community action groups.

The problems of maintaining effective community mediation in Lebanon and implementing community mediation in the United States are administratively and culturally different. Implementation and maintenance of community alternatives to courts involves culturally specific adaptations to community characteristics. The support of lawyers and the legal profession, for example, is necessary for prolonged success of local mediation in both the American and Lebanese setting, but different organizational tactics would be necessary to mobilize these two professional groups—the needs, demands, expectations, and cultural temperaments of legal professionals in the two societies are quite different. The theory of mediation allows comparison and prediction of the success of community mediation, regardless of the administrative specificity of particular programs.

The principles of mediation explain the necessary personal and local prerequisites for successful mediation. Summarily, they deal with what people must minimally believe, how the vested interests must be balanced, and how the relative benefits and costs of local, private settlements are weighed by individuals.

The theoretical propositions deal with the larger social conditions that must be fostered or must preexist for successful mediation to occur. The propositions thereby set forth the social parameters within which mediation will or will not work. The degree of on-going social interaction and reciprocity between members of a society, the degree of cultural distance, the extent of social stratification, and the range of mediation principles present in a social group will predictively determine the viability of mediation as a community process. The theory of mediation also posits a universal relationship between mediation and law in which both are complimentary but divergent systems of dispute resolution with different origins and goals.

The theory would be seriously challenged by a society with minimal interpersonal interaction and reciprocity where mediation was the rule, or by a traditional community with high interaction, reciprocity, kin obligations, and shared community values where adjudication was the preferred form of dispute settlement in local communities. A survey of the ethnographic data generated the theory as it is now formulated, and it further highlights the developmental patterns of law and mediation in a number of culturally disparate societies.

Although planning for the development of legal institutions is a process often rejected for application to third world countries in the throes of rapid economic development and change, an important aspect of the theory of mediation is that it shows the similarities of the American community and legal experience with the third world cases, as well as the differences. The thrust of the argument generated by the theory of mediation is that the American legal system and American communities are also growing and changing in a definite but undirected fashion. The theory presents ideas, cross-cultural case materials, and prediction hypotheses that are applicable to the understanding of legal development questions in any society, and to the implementation of mediational alternatives in American society in a responsive and informal process of change.

References

Abu-Loghod, J.
- 1961 Migrant adjustment to city life: the Egyptian case. *American Journal of Sociology* 68: 22–32.
- 1965 Urbanization in Egypt: present state and future prospects. *Economic Development and Culture Change* 13: 313–343.

Alinsky, S.
- 1969 *Reveille for radicals*. New York: Random House. [First published 1946.]
- 1971 *Rules for radicals: a practical primer for realistic radicals*. New York: Random House.

Anderson, J. N. D.
- 1954 The Shari'a and civil law. *The Islamic Quarterly* 1: 29–46.
- 1959 *Islamic law in the modern world*. New York: New York Univ. Press.
- 1965a Recent reforms in the Islamic law of inheritance. *International and Comparative Law Quarterly* 14: 349–365.
- 1965b The adaptation of Muslim law in sub-Saharan Africa." In *African law*, edited by H. Kuper and L. Kuper. Berkeley: Univ. of California Press.
- 1971 Modern trends in Islam: legal reform and modernization in the Middle East. *International and Comparative Law Quaterly* 20: 1–21.

Antoun, R. T.
- 1965 Conservatism and change in a village community: a Jordanian case study. *Human Organization* 24: 4–10.
- 1967 Social organization and the life cycle in an Arab village. *Ethnology* 6(3): 294–308.
- 1968a On the significance of names in an Arab village. *Ethnology* 7(2): 158–170.
- 1968b On the modesty of women in Arab villages: a study in the accommodation of traditions. *American Anthropoligist* 70: 671–697.

Aubert, V.
- 1969 Law as a way of resolving conflicts: the case of a small industrialized society. In *Law in culture and society*, edited by L. Nader. Chicago: Aldine.

Auerbach, J.
- 1969 Legal development in developing countries: the American experience. *American Society of International Law Proceedings.* 63: 81–90.
- 1976 *Unequal justice: law and social change in modern America.* New York: Oxford Univ. Press.

Ayoub, M. R.
- 1959 Parallel cousin marriage and endogamy: a study in sociometry. *Southwestern Journal of Anthropoligy* 15(3): 266–275.

Ayoub, V.
- 1965 Conflict resolution and social re-organization in a Lebanese village. *Human Organization* 24: 11–17.

Bahr, H. M., and G. R. Garett
- 1976 *Women alone: the disaffiliation of urban females.* Lexington, Mass.: Lexington Books.

Bailey, F. G.
- 1960 *Tribe, caste, and nation: a study of political activity and political change in highland Orissa.* Manchester,: Manchester Univ. Press.
- 1965 Decisions by consensus in councils and communities. In *Political systems and the distribution of power,* edited by M. Banton, A.S.A. Monograph No. 2. London: Tavistock.
- 1969 *Strategems and spoils.* New York: Schocken.

Bailey, F. G. (Ed.)
- 1971 *Gifts and poison: the politics of reputation.* Oxford: Basil Blackwell.
- 1973 *Debate and compromise: the politics of innovation.* Oxford: Basil Blackwell.

Banton, M. (Ed.)
- 1965a *Political systems and the distribution of power.* London: Tavistock.
- 1965b *The relevance of models for social anthropology.* A.S.A. Monograph No. 1. London: Tavistock.

Barclay, H.
- 1964 *Buuri al-Lamaab.* Ithaca, N.Y.: Cornell Univ. Press.

Barnes, J. A.
- 1954 Class and committees in a Norwegian island parish. *Human Relations* 7: 39–58.
- 1961 Law as politically active: an anthropological view. In *Studies in the sociology of law,* edited by G. Sawer. Canberra: Australian National Univ.
- 1969a Graph theory and social networks: a technical comment on connectedness and connectivity. *Sociology* 3: 215–232.
- 1969b Networks and political process. In *Social networks in urban situations,* edited by J. C. Mitchell. Manchester,: Manchester Univ. Press.

Barth, F.
- 1953 *Principles of social organization in Southern Kurdistan.* Universities Ethnografiske Museum (Oslo), Bulletin No. 7. Oslo, Norway: Brodrene Jorgensen.
- 1954 Father's brother's daughter marriage in Kurdistan. *Southwestern Journal of Anthropology* 10(2): 164–171.
- 1959a *Political leadership among Swat Pathans.* London School of Economics Monographs on Social Anthropology No. 19. New York: Humanities Press.
- 1959b Segmentary opposition and the theory of games. *Journal of the Royal Anthropological Institute* 89(1): 5–21.
- 1961 *Nomads of South Persia.* Boston: Little, Brown.
- 1963 *The role of the entrepreneur in social change in Northern Norway.* Bergen, Norway: Universitetsforlaget.
- 1966 *Models of social organization.* Royal Anthropological Institute of Great Britain and Ireland, Occasional Papers No. 23. London: Royal Anthropological Institute.

1969 *Ethnic groups and boundaries: the social organization of cultural differences.* London: Allen and Unwin.
1973 Descent and marriage reconsidered. In *The character of kinship*, edited by J. Goody. London: Cambridge Univ. Press.

Barton, R. F.
1919 *Ifugao law.* University of California Publications in American Archaeology and Ethnology 15: 1-186. [Reprinted 1969.] Berkeley and Los Angeles: Univ. of California Press.
1949 *The Kalingas: their institutions and custom law.* Chicago: Univ. of Chicago Press.

Bateson, G.
1936 *Naven.* Cambridge: Harvard University Press.
1958 Epilogue. In *Naven.* (2nd ed.) Stanford: Stanford Univ. Press.

Beattie, J.
1957 Informal judicial activity in Bunyoro. *Journal of African Administration* 9(4): 188-195.

Beck, M. A.
1977 *Alternative approaches to dispute resolution.* National Institute of Law Enforcement and Criminal Justice. Unpublished manuscript.

Beck, L., and N. Keddie (Eds.)
1978 *Women in the Muslim world.* Cambridge: Harvard University Press.

Befu, H.
1963 Network and corporate structure: a structural approach to community inter-relations in Japan. In *Studies on Asia*, edited by R. K. Sakai. Lincoln: Univ. of Nebraska Press.
1967 The political relation of the village to the state. *World Politics* 29: 67-95.

Benedict, B.
1962 Stratification in plural societies. *American Anthropologist* 64(6): 1235-1246.
1965 *Mauritius: Problems of a plural society.* London: Pall Mall Press.
1968 Small societies. In *International encyclopedia of the social sciences*, edited by D. Sills. 14: 572-577. New York: Macmillan and Free Press.

Black, D.
1970 Production of crime rates. *American Sociological Review* 35: 733-748.
1971 The social organization of arrest. *Stanford Law Review* 23: 1087-1111.
1973 The mobilization of law. *Journal of Legal Studies* 2: 125-149.
1976 *The behavior of law.* New York: Academic.

Black, D., and M. Mileski (Eds.)
1973 *The social organization of law.* New York: Seminar.

Blauner, R.
1964 *Alienation and freedom.* Chicago: Univ. of Chicago Press.
1972b Black culture: myth or reality. In *White racism and black Americans*, edited by D. G. Bromley and C. F. Longion, Jr. Cambridge, Mass.: Schenkman.
1972b *Racial oppression in America.* New York: Harper & Row.

Blok, A.
1969 Variations in patronage. *Sociologishe Gids* 16: 365-378.
1973 Coalitions in Sicilian peasant society. In *Network analysis: studies in human interaction*, edited by J. Boissevain and J. C. Mitchell. The Hague: Mouton.
1974 *The mafia of a Sicilian village, 1860-1960: a study of violent peasant entrepreneurs.* Oxford: Basil Blackwell.

Boissevain, J.
1964 Factions, parties, and politics in a Maltese village. *American Anthropologist* 66: 1275-1287.
1965 *Saints and fireworks: religion and politics in rural Malta.* London: Athlone.

1966 Patronage in Sicily. *Man* 1(1): 18–33.
1968 The place of non-groups in the social sciences. *Man* 3: 542–556.
1969a *Hal-Farrug: a village in Malta*. New York: Holt.
1969b Patrons as brokers. *Sociologishe Gids* 16: 379–386.
1971 Second thoughts on quasi-groups, categories and coalitions. *Man* 6: 468–472.
1973 An exploration of two first-order zones. In *Network analysis: studies in human interaction*, edited by J. Boissevain and J. C. Mitchell. The Hague: Mouton.
1974 *Friends of friends: networks, manipulators, and coalitions*. Oxford: Basil Blackwell.

Boserup, E.
1970 *Women's role in economic development*. London: Allen and Unwin.

Bott, E.
1971 *Family and social networks*. London: Tavistock.

Brickman, L.
1973 Of arterial passageways through the legal process: the right of universal access to courts and lawyering services. *New York University Law Review* 48: 595–668.

Briggs, L.
1960 *Tribes of the Sahara*. Cambridge, Mass.: Harvard Univ. Press.

Bujra, A. S.
1971 *The politics of stratification: a study of political change in a South Arabian town*. Oxford: Clarendon Press.

Byles, A., and P. Morris
1977 *Unmet need: the case of the neighbourhood law centre*. London: Routledge & Kegan Paul.

Cahn, E. S., and J. C. Cahn.
1964 Implementing the civilian perspective: a proposal for a neighborhood law firm. *Yale Law Journal* 73: 1317–1352.
1966 What price justice? The civilian perspective revisited. Symposium: Justice and the Poor. *Notre Dame Lawyer* 41: 927–960.
1970 Power to the people or the profession? The public interest in Public Interest Law. *Yale Law Journal* 79: 1005–1048.

Cappelletti, M.
1976 Toward equal justice: a comparative study. *Michigan Law Review* 73: 794–884.

Champagne, A.
1976 Legal services: an exploratory study in effectiveness. *Administrative and Policy Studies* 3: 5–23.

Chelhod, J.
1965 Le mariage avec le cousin parallele dons le systeme Arabe. *L'Homme* 9: 24–40.

Chestang, L.
1972 *Character development in a hostile environment*. Occasional Paper No. 3. Chicago: Univ. of Chicago Press, School of Social Service Administration.
1976a Environmental influences on social functioning: the Black experience. In *The diverse society: implications for social policy*, edited by L. Chestang and P. Cafferty. New York: Association Press.
1976b The Black family and Black culture: a study in coping. In *Cross cultural perspectives in social work practice and education*, edited by M. Sotomayer. Houston: Univ. of Houston, Press, Graduate School of Social Work.

Cloward, R., and F. Piven
1974 *The politics of turmoil: essays on poverty, race, and the urban crisis*. New York: Pantheon.
1977 *Poor people's movements: why they succeed, how they fail*. New York: Vintage Books, Random House.

Cochrane, G.
 1971 *Development anthropology.* London: Oxford Univ. Press.
Cohen, A.
 1965 *Arab border villages in Israel: a study of continuity and change in social organization.* Manchester: Manchester Univ. Press.
Cohen, J. A.
 1967 Chinese mediation on the eve of modernization. In *Traditional and modern legal institutions in Asia and Africa,* edited by D. C. Buxbaum. Leiden: Brill.
Cohen, Y. A.
 1964 The establishment of identity in a social nexus: the special case of initiation ceremonies and their relation to value and legal systems. *American Anthropologist* 66: 522-529.
Cole, D.
 1971 *The social and economic structure of the Al-Murrah: a Saudi Arabian Bedouin tribe.* Ph.D. dissertation, University of California, Berkeley.
 1973 The enmeshment of nomads in Saudi Arabian society: the case of the Al-Murrah. In *The desert and the sown: nomads in the wider society,* edited by C. Nelson, Berkeley: Institute of International Studies.
 1975 *Nomads of the nomads: the Al-Murrah tribe of the empty quarter.* Chicago: Aldine.
Collier, J. F.
 1973 *Law and social change in Zinacantan.* Stanford: Stanford Univ. Press.
 1977 Political leadership and legal change in Zinacantan. *Law and Society Review* 11: 131-163.
 1979 Stratification and dispute handling in two highland Chiapas communites. *American Ethnologist* 6(2); 305-328.
Collins, A., and D. L. Pancoast
 1976 *Natural helping networks: a strategy for prevention.* Washington, D.C.: National Association of Social Workers.
Colson, E.
 1953 Social control and vengeance in Plateau Tonga society. *Africa* 23: 199-212.
 1967 The intensive study of small sample communities. In *The craft of social anthropology,* edited by A. L. Epstein. London: Tavistock.
 1974 *Tradition and contract: the problem of order.* Chicago: Aldine.
Coon, C.
 1958 *Caravan: the story of the Middle East.* New York: Holt.
Cornu, G.
 1951 *Etude comparee de la responsabilité delictuelle en droit privee et en droit public.* Reims: Matot-Braine.
Coulson, N. J.
 1964 *A history of Islamic law.* Edinburgh: Edinburgh Univ. Press.
 1969 *Conflicts and tensions in Islamic jurisprudence.* Chicago: Univ. Chicago Press.
Cramton, R. C.
 1975 The task ahead in legal services. *American Bar Association Journal* 61: 1339-1343.
Cunnison, I.
 1966 *Baggara Arabs: power and the lineage in a Sudanese nomad tribe.* Oxford: Clarendon Press.
Curran, B. A., and F. Spalding
 1974 *The legal needs of the public: a preliminary report.* Chicago: American Bar Association and American Bar Foundation.
Danzig, R., and M. J. Lowy
 1975 Everyday disputes and mediation in the United States: a reply to Professor Felstiner. *Law and Society Review* 9(4): 675-94.

Deng, F. M.
  1971 *Tradition and modernization: a challenge for law among the Dinka of the Sudan.* New Haven: Yale Univ. Press.
Dickson, F. R. P.
  1951 *The Arab of the desert: a glimpse into life in Kuwait and Saudi Arabia.* London: Allen and Unwin.
Doo, L. W.
  1973 Dispute settlement in Chinese-American communities. *American Journal of Comparative Law* 21: 650–663.
Doumani, O.
  1974 *Tobacco growers of southern Lebanon: the politics and economics of change.* Ph.D. dissertation, University of California, Berkeley.
du Boulay, J.
  1974 *Portrait of a Greek mountain village.* Oxford: Clarendon Press.
Durkheim, E.
  1954 *The elementary forms of the religious life.* London: Allen and Unwin. Originally published 1911.
Duvignaud, J.
  1970 *Change at Shebika: report from a North African village.* New York: Pantheon.
Dwyer, D.
  1977 Bridging the gap between the sexes in Moroccan legal practice. In *Sexual stratification: a cross-cultural view,* edited by A. Schlegal. New York: Columbia University Press.
  1979 Law actual and perceived: the sexual politics of law in Morocco. *Law and Society Review* 13(3): 739–756.
Ehrenfels, U. B.
  1949 History of womanhood in Islamic society: the real meaning of the claim that Islam is the first social order to regard woman as an entity in her own right. *The Islamic Review* 37: 31–36.
Eisenstadt, S. N.
  1965 *Essays on comparative institutions.* New York: Wiley.
Elias, N., and J. L. Scotson
  1965 *The established and the outsiders: a sociological enquiry into community problems.* London: Frank Cass.
Epstein, A. L.
  1961 The network and urban social organization. *Rhodes-Livingstone Journal* 29: 29–62.
  1974 *Contention and dispute: aspects of law and social control in Malanesia.* Canberra: Australian National Univ. Press.
Evans-Pritchard, E. E.
  1940 *The Nuer.* Oxford: Clarendon Press.
  1949 *The Sanusi of Cyrenaica.* Oxford: Clarendon Press.
Fakhouri, H.
  1972 *Kafr el-Elow: an Egyptian village in transition.* New York: Holt.
Fallers, L.
  1964 *The king's men: leadership and status in Buganda on the eve of independence.* London: Oxford Univ. Press.
Feldstein, S., and L. Costello (Eds.)
  1974 *The ordeal of assimilation: a documentary history of the white working class.* New York: Anchor.
Felstiner, W. L. F.
  1974 Influences of social organization on dispute processing. *Law and Society Review* 9(1): 63–94.

References

    1975   Avoidance as dispute processing: an elaboration. *Law and Society Review* 9(4): 695–706.

Fernea, R. A.
- 1970 *Shaykh and effendi: changing patterns of authority among the El Shabana of southern Iraq.* Cambridge, Mass.: Harvard Univ. Press.
- 1972 Gaps in the ethnographic literature on the Middle Eastern village: a classificatory exploration. In *Rural politics and social change in the Middle East*, edited by R. Antoun and I. Harik. Bloomington: Indiana Univ. Press.

Fernea, R. A., and J. A. Malarkey
- 1975 Anthropology of the Middle East and North Africa: a critical assessment. In *Annual review of anthropology*, vol. 4, edited by B. J. Siegel. Palo Alto, Calif.: Annual Review.

Firth, R.
- 1951 *Elements of social organization.* London: Watts.
- 1957 Introduction. Symposium on factions in Indian and overseas Indian societies. *British Journal of Sociology* 8: 291–295.
- 1964 *Essays on social organization and values.* London School of Economics Monograph in Social Anthropology No. 28. London: Athlone.

Forman, S.
- 1972 *Law and conflict in rural highland Ecuador.* Ph.D. dissertation, University of California, Berkeley.

Fortes, M.
- 1949 *The web of kinship among the Tallensi.* London: Oxford Univ. Press.
- 1953 The structure of unilineal descent groups. *American Anthropologist* 55: 17–41.

Franck, T. (Ed.)
- 1968 *Why federations fail.* New York: New York Univ. Press.

Frankenberg, R. J.
- 1957 *Village on the border.* London: Cohen & West.

Frey, F. W.
- 1965 *The Turkish political elite.* Cambridge, Mass.: M.I.T. Press.

Friedman, L. M., and R. V. Percival
- 1976 A tale of two courts: litigation in Alameda and San Benito counties. *Law and Society Review* 10(2): 267–301.

Friedrich, C. J.
- 1968 *Trends of federalism in theory and practice.* New York: Praeger.

Fuller, A.
- 1961 *Buarij: portrait of a Lebanese Muslim village.* Harvard Middle Eastern Monographs No. 6. Cambridge, Mass.: Harvard Univ. Press.

Fuller, L.
- 1968 *The anatomy of law.* New York: Praeger.

Galanter, M.
- 1974 Why the "haves come out ahead": speculations on the limits of legal change. *Law and Society Review* 9(1): 95–160.
- 1976 Delivering legality: some proposals for the direction of research. *Law and Society Review* 11(2): 225–246.

Gans, H.
- 1961 *The urban villagers: group and class in the life of Italian-Americans.* New York: Free Press.
- 1974 Mean streets: a study of the young working class. *Social Policy* 4: 61–62.

Geertz, C.
- 1963 The integrative revolution: primordial sentiments and civil politics in the new states. In *Old societies and new states: the quest for modernity in Asia and Africa*, edited by C. Geertz. New York: Free Press.

Gellner, E.
  1969 *Saints of the atlas.* Chicago: Chicago Univ. Press.
Gibbs, J. L., Jr.
  1962 Poro values and courtroom procedures in a Kpelle chiefdom. *Southwestern Journal of Anthropology* 18: 341-351.
  1963 The Kpelle moot: a therapeutic model for the informal settlement of disputes. *Africa* 33: 1-11.
  1969 Law and personality: signposts for a new direction. In *Law in culture and society*, edited by L. Nader. Chicago: Aldine.
  1973 Two forms of dispute settlement among the Kpelle of west Africa. In *The social organization of law*, edited by D. Black and M. Mileski. New York: Seminar.
Gluckman, M.
  1955 *The judicial process among the Barotse of northern Rhodesia.* Manchester: Manchester University Press.
  1965 *The ideas in Barotse jurisprudence.* New Haven: Yale Univ. Press.
Gonzalez, N. L.
  1973 Patron-client relationships at the international level. In *Structure and process in Latin America*, edited by A. Strickon. Albuquerque: Univ. of New Mexico Press.
Granquist, H.
  1931 *Marriage conditions in a Palestinian village.* Helsinki, Finland: Societas Scientiarum Fennica.
Guilick, J. A.
  1953a The Lebanese village: an introduction. *American Anthropologist* 55: 367-372.
  1953b Conservation and change in a Lebanese village. *Middle East Journal* 8(3): 295-307.
  1955 *Social structure and culture change in a Lebanese village.* Viking Fund Publication in Anthropology No. 21. New York: Johnson Reprint Corp. Reprinted 1971.
  1963 Images of an Arab city. *Journal of the American Institute of Planners* 24: 179-198.
  1967 *Tripoli: a modern Arab city.* Cambridge, Mass.: Harvard Univ. Press.
  1976 *The Middle East: an anthropological perspective.* Pacific Palisades, Calif.: Goodyear.
Gulliver, P. H.
  1963 *Social control in an African society: a study of the Arusha, agricultural Masai of Northern Tanganyika.* Boston: Boston Univ. Press.
  1971 *Neighbours and networks: the idiom of kinship in social action among the Ndendeuli of Tanzania.* Berkeley: Univ. of California Press.
  1977 On mediators. In *Social anthropology and law*, edited by I. Hamnet. A.S.A. Monograph 14. New York: Academic.
Haas, E. B.
  1971 The study of regional integration: reflection on the joy and anguish of pretheorizing. In *Regional integration*, edited by L. N. Lindberg and S. H. Scheingold. Cambridge: Harvard Univ. Press.
Hahm, P.
  1967 *The Korean political tradition and law.* Seoul, Korea: Hollym Corporation Publishers.
  1968 Korea's initial encounter with western law: 1866-1910 A.D. *Korea Observer* 1: 80-93.
Handler, J., E. J. Hollingsworth, and H. S. Erlanger
  1978 *Lawyers and the pursuit of legal rights.* New York: Academic.
Hannerz, U.
  1969 *Soulside: inquiries into ghetto culture and community.* New York: Columbia Univ. Press.
Hart, D. B.
  1973 The tribe in modern Morocco: two case studies. In *Arabs and Berbers: from tribe to nation in Africa*, edited by E. Gellner and C. Micaud. London: Duckworth.

References

Henderson, D. F.
   1965 *Conciliation and Japanese law.* 2 vol. Seattle: Univ. of Washington Press.

Hirshman, A. O.
   1970 *Exit, voice and loyalty: responses to decline in firms, organizations and states.* Cambridge, Mass.: Harvard Univ. Press.

Hoebel, E. A.
   1968 *The law of primitive man.* New York: Antheneum. [Originally published by Harvard Univ. Press, 1954.]

Howell, J. T.
   1973 *Hard living on Clay Street.* New York: Anchor.

Hudson, M. C.
   1968 *The precarious republic: political modernization in Lebanon.* New York: Random House.

Huntington, S. P.
   1968 *Political order in changing societies.* New Haven: Yale Univ. Press.

Jones, S.
   1974 *Men of influence in Nuristan: a study of social control and dispute settlement in Waigal Valley, Afghanistan.* New York: Seminar.

Jongmans, D. G.
   1973 Politics on the village level. In *Network analysis: studies in human interaction*, edited by J. Boissevain and J. C. Mitchell. The Hague: Mouton.

Kanaan, A. J.
   1972 *The political economy of development planning: the case of Lebanon.* Ph.D. dissertation, University of California, Berkeley.

Katz, P. S.
   1975 Village responses to national law: a case from the South Tyrol. In *Beyond the community: social process in Europe*, edited by J. Boissevain and J. Friedl. The Hague: European-Mediterranean Study Group of the University of Amsterdam.

Kawashima, T.
   1973 Dispute settlement in Japan. In *The social organization of law*, edited by D. Black and M. Mileski. New York: Seminar.

Kennett, A.
   1968 *Bedouin justice: law and customs among the Egyptian bedouin.* London: Frank Cass.

Khuri, F.
   1968 The etiquette of bargaining in the Middle East. *American Anthropologist* 70: 698–706.
   1970 Parallel cousin marriage reconsidered: a Middle Eastern practice that nullifies the effects of marriage on the intensity of family relationships. *Man* 5: 597–618.
   1975 *From village to suburb: order and change in greater Beirut.* Chicago: Univ. of Chicago Press.

Klonoski, J. F., and R. I. Mendelsohn
   1970 *The politics of local justice.* Boston: Little, Brown.

Kolars, J. F.
   1967 Types of rural development. In *Four studies on the economic development of Turkey*, edited by F. C. Shorter. London: Frank Cass.

Kornblum, W.
   1974 *Blue collar community.* Chicago: Univ. of Chicago Press.

Kuper, H., and L. Kuper (Eds.)
   1965 *African law: adaptation and development.* Berkeley: Univ. of California Press.

Kuper, L., and M. G. Smith
   1971 *Pluralism in Africa.* Berkeley: Univ. of California Press.

Ladner, J.
  1971 *Tomorrow's tomorrow*. New York: Anchor.
Lapidus, I.
  1967 *Muslim cities in the later middle ages*. Cambridge, Mass.: Harvard Univ. Press.
Leach, E. R.
  1940 *Social and economic organization of the Rowanduz Kurds*. London: Percy Lund, Humphries.
  1953 Bridewealth and the stability of marriage. *Man* 53: 179–180.
Lempert, R.
  1978 More tales of two courts: exploring changes in the "dispute settlement function" of trial courts. *Law and Society Review* 13(1): 91–138.
Lerner, D., and M. Gorden
  1969 *Euratlantica: changing perspectives of the European elites*. Cambridge, Mass.: M.I.T. Press.
Lerner, M. P.
  1979 Surplus powerlessness. *Social Policy* 9(4): 18–27.
Levi-Strauss, C.
  1953 Social structure. In *Structural anthropology*. New York: Basic Books. [Republished 1963.]
  1964 Reciprocity: the essence of social life. In *The family: its structure and function*, edited by R. L. Coser. New York: St Martin's.
Levitan, S. (Ed.)
  1971 *Blue collar workers: a symposium on middle America*. New York: McGraw-Hill.
Lieberman, J. K.
  1970 *The tyranny of experts: how professionals are closing the open society*. New York: Walker.
Lindberg, L. N., and S. A. Scheingold (Eds.)
  1971 *Regional integration. theory and research*. Cambridge, Mass.: Harvard Univ. Press.
Lutfiyya, A. M.
  1966 *Baytin: a Jordanian village*. The Hague: Mouton.
Macaulay, S.
  1963 Non-contractual relations in business: a preliminary study. *American Sociological Review* 28: 55–66.
Magavern, J. L., J. Thomas, and M. Stuart
  1975 Law, urban development, and the poor in developing countries. *Washington University Law Quarterly* 1: 45–111.
Magnarella, P. G., and O. Turkdogan
  1973 Descent, affinity, and ritual relations in Eastern Turkey. *American Anthropologist* 75(5): 1626–1633.
  1974 *Tradition and change in a Turkish town*. New York: Wiley.
Maher, V.
  1974 *Woman and property in Morocco: their changing relation to the process of social strategy in the Middle Atlas*. Cambridge: Cambridge Univ. Press.
Malinowski, B.
  1926 *Crime and custom in savage society*. London: Kegan Paul, Trench, Trubner.
Mangin, W. (Ed.)
  1970 *Peasants in cities: readings in the anthropology of urbanization*. Boston: Houghton Mifflin.
Marks, F. R.
  1971 *The legal needs of the poor: a critical analysis*. Chicago: American Bar Association.
  1976 Some research perspectives for looking at legal need and legal service delivery systems: old forms or new? *Law and Society Review* 11: 191–105.

References

Martin, E. P., and J. M. Martin
  1978 *The Black extended family.* Chicago: Univ. of Chicago Press.
Marx, E.
  1967 *Bedouin of the Negev.* New York: Praeger.
  1977 The tribe as a unit of subsistence: nomadic pastoralism in the Middle East. *American Anthropologist* 79(2): 343-363.
Massell, G. J.
  1968 Law as an instrument of revolutionary change in a traditional milieu: the case of Soviet Central Asia. *Law and Society Review* 2: 179-228.
Mather, L. M.
  1977 Ethnography and the study of trial courts. In *Public law and public policy*, edited by J. A. Gardiner. New York: Praeger.
Mauss, M.
  1906 *The gift: forms and functions of exchange in archaic societies.* New York: Norton. [Reprinted 1967.]
Mayhew, L. H.
  1968 *Law and equal opportunity: a study of the Massachusetts Commission against Discrimination.* Cambridge, Mass.: Harvard Univ. Press.
  1975 Institutions of representatives: civil justice and the public. *Law and Society Review* 9: 401-429.
Mayhew, L. H., and A. J. Reiss
  1969 The social organization of legal contacts. *American Sociological Review* 34: 309-318.
Mayer, A. C.
  1966 The significance of quasi-groups in the study of complex societies. In *The social anthropology of complex societies*, edited by M. Banton. London: Tavistock.
Mayer, P.
  1971 *Townsmen or tribesmen: conservatism and the process of urbanization in a South African city.* London: Oxford Univ. Press.
Mayfield, J. B.
  1971 *Rural politics in Nasser's Egypt: a quest for legitimacy.* Austin: Univ. of Texas Press.
McKenzie, H. I.
  1966 The plural society debate: some comments on a recent contribution. *Social and Economic Studies* 15(1): 53-60.
Mernissi, F.
  1975 *Beyond the veil: male-female dynamics in a modern Muslim society.* Cambridge: Schenkman.
Mileski, M.
  1971 Courtroom encounters: an observational study of a lower criminal court. *Law and Society Review* 5(4): 473-538.
Mitchell, J. C.
  1971 The concept and use of social networks. In *Social networks in urban situations: analyses of personal relationships in central African towns*, edited by J. C. Mitchell. Manchester: Manchester Univ. Press.
Moore, W., Jr.
  1961 *The vertical ghetto: everyday life in an urban project.* New York: Random House.
Morris, H. S.
  1967 Some aspects of the concept plural society. *Man* 2(2): 169-184.
Moynihan, D. P.
  1969 *Maximum feasible misunderstanding: community action and the war on poverty.* New York: Free Press.

Muench, G. A. A.
  1963 A clinical psychologist's treatment of labor-management disputes. *Journal of Humanistic Psychology* 3: 92–97.
Muhyi, I. A.
  1959 Women in the Arab Middle East. *Journal of Social Issues* 15(3): 45–57.
Murphy, R. F.
  1971 *The dialects of social life. Alarms and excursions in anthropological theory.* New York: Basic Books.
Murphy, R. F., and L. Kasdan
  1959 The structure of parallel cousin marriage. *American Anthropologist* 61: 17–29.
  1967 Agnation and endogamy: some further considerations. *Southwestern Journal of Anthropology* 21: 325–505.
Musil, A.
  1928 *The manners and customs of the Rwala Bedouins.* Oriental Explorations and Studies No. 6. New York: American Geographical Society.
Mustafa, Z.
  1971 *The common law in the Sudan: an account of the justice, equity, and good conscience provision.* Oxford: Clarendon Press.
Nader, L.
  1965a Choices in legal procedure: Shia Moslem and Mexican Zapotec. *American Anthropologist* 67: 394–399.
  1965b Communication between village and city in the modern Middle East. *Human Organization* 24: 18–24.
  1965c The anthropological study of law. *American Anthropologist* 67(6)(2): 3–32.
  1969 Styles of court procedure: to make the balance. In *Law in culture and society*, edited by L. Nader. Chicago: Aldine.
Nader, L., and L. Singer
  1976 Dispute resolution in the future: what are the choices. *California State Bar Journal* 51: 281–320.
Nader, L., and H. F. Todd, Jr. (Eds.)
  1978 *The disputing process: law in ten societies.* New York: Columbia Univ. Press.
Nader, L., and B. Yngvesson
  1974 On studying the ethnography of law and its consequences. In *Handbook of social and cultural anthropology*, edited by J. J. Honigman. Chicago: Rand McNally.
Nader, L. et al.
  1979 *Consumption, location and occupation patterns group report*, edited by L. Nader. Committee on Nuclear and Alternative Energy Systems. Washington, D.C.: National Academy of Sciences.
Nelson, C.
  1973 Women and power in nomadic societies in the Middle East. In *The desert and the sown: nomads in the wider society*, edited by C. Nelson. Berkeley: Institute of International Studies.
Nevins, E.
  1969 *World without time: the bedouin.* New York: John Day.
Nicholas, R. W.
  1965 Factions: a comparative analysis. In *Political systems and the distribution of power*, edited by M. Banton. A.S.A. Monograph No. 2. London: Tavistock.
  1966 Segmentary factional political systems. In *Political anthropology*, edited by M. Swartz, V. Turner, and A. Tuden. Chicago: Aldine.

References

Norton, D.
  1976 Residential environment and Black self-image. In *The diverse society: implications for social policy*, edited by P. Cafferty and L. Chestang. Washington, D.C.: National Association of Social Workers.
Norton, D. et al.
  1978 *The dual perspective: inclusion of ethnic minority content in the social work curriculum.* New York: Council on Social Work Education.
Obermeyer, G. J.
  1973 Leadership and transition in Bedouin society: a case study. In *The desert and the sown: nomads in the wider society*, edited by C. Nelson. Berkeley: Institute of International Studies.
O'Connor, K. K.
  1977 Treatment for adults with psychosomatic symptoms. *Health and Social Work* 2(4): 89–111.
Packer, H. L.
  1968 *The limits of the criminal sanction.* Stanford: Stanford Univ. Press.
Patai, R.
  1951a Relationship patterns among the Arabs. *Middle Eastern Affairs* 2: 180–185.
  1951b Nomadism: Middle Eastern and Central Asian. *Southwestern Journal of Anthropology* 7(4): 401–414.
  1955 Cousin-right in Middle Eastern marriage. *Southwestern Journal of Anthropology* 11(4): 371–390.
  1965 The structure of endogamous unilineal descent groups. *Southwestern Journal of Anthropology* 21(4): 325–350.
Pehrson, R. N.
  1966 *The social organization of the Marri Baluch.* Chicago: Chicago Univ. Press.
Peters, E.
  1960 The proliferation of segments in the lineage of the Bedouin in Cyrenaica. *Journal of the Royal Anthropological Institute* 90: 29–53.
  1963 Aspects of rank and status among Muslims in a Lebanese village. In *Mediterranean countrymen*, edited by J. Pitt-Rivers. Leiden: Mouton.
  1965 Aspects of the family among the Bedouin of Cyrenaica. In *Comparative family systems*, edited by M. F. Nimkoff. Boston: Houghton Mifflin.
  1968 The tied and the free: an account of patron-client relationships among the Bedouin of Cyrenaica. In *Contributions to Mediterranean sociology*, edited by J. Peristiany. The Hague: Mouton.
  1977 Patronage in Cyrenaica. In *Patrons and clients*, edited by E. Gellner and J. Waterbury. London: Duckworth.
Pierce, J. E.
  1964 *Life in a Turkish village.* New York: Holt.
Pitt-Rivers, J. (Ed.)
  1963 *Mediterranean countrymen: essays in the social anthropology of the Mediterranean.* Paris: Mouton.
Peristiany, J. G. (Ed.)
  1966 *Honour and shame: the values of Mediterranean society.* Chicago: Univ. of Chicago Press.
Pospisil, L.
  1967 Legal levels and multiplicity of legal systems in human societies. *Journal of Conflict Resolution* 11(1): 2–26.
  1969 Structural change and primitive law: consequences of a Papuan legal case. In *Law in culture and society*, edited by L. Nader. Chicago: Aldine.
  1971 *Anthropology of law: a comparative theory.* New Haven: Yale Univ. Press.

Pound, R.
  1906 The causes of popular dissatisfaction with the administration of justice. *Reports of the American Bar Association* 29(1): 295–417.
Puchala, D. J.
  1968 The pattern of contemporary regional integration. *International Studies Quarterly* 12(1): 38–64.
Quandt, W. B.
  1970 The comparative study of political elites. *Sage Professional Papers in Comparative Politics* 1: 188–213.
Rabin, R. L.
  1976 Lawyers for social change: perspectives on public interest law. *Stanford Law Review* 28: 207–261.
Radcliffe-Brown, A. R.
  1935 Patrilineal and matrilineal succession. In *Structure and function in primitive society: essays and addresses by A. R. Radcliffe-Brown.* Glencoe, Ill.: Free Press.
Rein, M.
  1976 *Social science and public policy.* New York: Penguin.
Rosaldo, M., and L. Lamphere (Eds.)
  1974 *Woman, culture, and society.* Stanford: Stanford Univ. Press.
Rosenfield, H.
  1958a Processes of structural change with the Arab village extended family. *American Anthropologist* 60: 1127–1137.
  1958b An analysis of marriage and marriage statistics for a Muslim and Christian Arab village. *International Archives of Ethnography* 48: Part II.
Roos, L. L., and N. P. Roos
  1971 *Managers of modernization: organizations and elites in Turkey (1950–1969).* Cambridge, Mass.: Harvard Univ. Press.
Rosenberg, M.
  1971 Devising procedures that are civil to promote justice that is civilized. *Michigan Law Review* 69: 797–820.
Ross, H. L.
  1970 *Settled out of court: the social process of insurance claims adjustment.* Chicago: Aldine.
Rothenberger, J. E.
  1970 Law and conflict resolution, politics and change in a Sunni Muslim village in Lebanon. Ph.D. dissertation, University of California, Berkeley.
  1978 The social dynamics of dispute settlement in a Sunni Muslim village in Lebanon. In *The disputing process: law in ten societies,* edited by L. Nader and H. F. Todd, Jr. New York: Columbia Univ. Press.
Rubin, L. B.
  1976 *Worlds of pain: life in the working class family.* New York: Basic Books.
Ruffini, J.
  1974 Alternative systems of conflict management in Sardinia. Ph.D. dissertation, University of California, Berkeley.
  1978 Disputing over livestock in Sardinia. In *The disputing process: law in ten societies,* edited by L. Nader and H. F. Todd, Jr. New York: Columbia Univ. Press.
Rustow, D. A.
  1966 The development of parties in Turkey. In *Political parties and political development,* edited by J. Palamkara and M. Weiner. Princeton, N.J.: Princeton Univ. Press.

References

Salim, S. M.
- 1962 *Marsh dwellers of the Euphrates delta.* London School of Economics Monographs No. 23. London: Athlone.

Salzman, P. C.
- 1974 Tribal chiefs as middlemen: the politics of encapsulation in the Middle East. *Anthropological Quarterly* 41: 203–211.

Sarat, A.
- 1976 Alternatives in dispute processing: litigation in a small claims court. *Law and Society Review* 10: 339–375.
- 1977 Studying American legal culture: an assessment of survey evidence. *Law and Society Review* 11(3): 427–488.

Sarat, A., and J. B. Grossman
- 1975 Courts and conflict resolution. *American Political Science Review* 69(4): 1200–1217.

Schacht, J.
- 1964 *An introduction to Islamic law.* Oxford: Clarendon Press.

Scheingold, S. A.
- 1974 *The politics of rights: lawyers, public policy and political change.* New Haven: Yale Univ. Press.

Schmidt, C. C.
- 1952 Mediation in Sweden. In *Meeting of Minds: a way to peace through mediation*, edited by E. Jackson. New York: McGraw-Hill.

Schneider, J.
- 1969 Of vigilance and virgins: honor, shame, and access to resources in Mediterranean societies. *Ethnology* 10: 1–24.

Schorger, W. D.
- 1969 Evolution of political forms in a North Moroccan village. *Anthropological Quarterly* 42: 263–268.

Schwartz, R. D. and J. C. Miller
- 1964 Legal evolution and societal complexity. *American Journal of Sociology* 70: 159–169.

Seligman, C. G. and B. Z. Seligman
- 1918 *The Kababish: a Sudan Arab tribe.* Harvard African Studies, Vol. 2. Cambridge, Mass.: Harvard Univ. Press.

Shibutani, T., and K. M. Kwan
- 1965 *Ethnic stratification: a comparative approach.* New York: Macmillan.

Simkin, W. E.
- 1971 *Mediation and the dynamic of collective bargaining.* Washington D.C.: Bureau of National Affairs.

Skolnick, A. S., and J. H. Skolnick (Eds.)
- 1971 *Family in transition.* Boston: Little, Brown.
- 1974 *Intimacy, family, and society.* Boston: Little, Brown.

Smith, R. H.
- 1919 *Justice and the poor.* New York: The Carnegie Foundation for the Advancement of Teaching.

Smith, W. R.
- 1903 *Kinship and marriage in early Arabia.* London: Adam and Charles Black.

Speck, R. V., and C. Attneare
- 1973 *Family networks.* New York: Random House.

Spence, J.
- 1978 Institutionalizing neighborhood courts: two Chilean experiences. *Law and Society Review* 13(1): 139–182.

Spiro, M.
- 1968 Factionalism and politics in village Burma. In *Local level politics*, edited by M. Swartz. Chicago: Aldine.

Spooner, B.
- 1973 *The cultural ecology of pastoral nomads.* Addison-Wesley Module in Anthropology No. 45. Reading, Mass.: Addison-Wesley.

Spradley, J. P.
- 1970 *You owe yourself a drunk: an ethnography of urban nomads.* Boston: Little, Brown.
- 1973 The ethnography of crime in American society. In *Cultural illness and health*, edited by L. Nader and T. Maretski. Washington, D.C.: American Anthropological Association.

Srinivas, M. N., and A. Beteille
- 1964 Networks in Indian social structure. *Man* 64: 165–168.

Srole, L., T. Langner, S. Michael, M. Opler, and T. Rennie
- 1962 *Mental health in the metropolis: the midtown Manhattan study.* New York: McGraw-Hill.

Stack, C.
- 1971 *All our kin.* New York: Harper & Row.

Starr, J.
- 1970 *Manda linci koy: law and social control in a Turkish village.* Ph.D. dissertation, University of California, Berkeley.
- 1978a *Dispute and settlement in rural Turkey: an ethnography of law.* Leiden: E. J. Brill.
- 1978b Turkish village disputing behavior. In *The disputing process: law in ten societies*, edited L. Nader and H. F. Todd, Jr. New York: Columbia Univ. Press.

Starr, J., and J. Pool
- 1974 The impact of a legal revolution in rural Turkey. *Law and Society Reviw* 8(4): 533–560.

Stirling, P.
- 1966 *Turkish village.* New York: Wiley.

Stumpf, H. P.
- 1975 *Community politics and legal services: the other side of the law.* Sage Series on Politcs and the Legal Order, Vol. 4. Beverly Hills, Calif.: Sage.

Sutherland, E.
- 1949 *White collar crime.* New York: Holt.

Suttles, G. D.
- 1968 *The social order of the slum.* Chicago: Univ. of Chicago Press.

Sweet, L.
- 1960 *Tell Toqaan: a Syrian village.* Anthropological Papers No. 14. Ann Arbor: Univ. of Michigan, Museum of Anthropology.
- 1965a Camel pastoralism in North Arabia and the minimal camping unit. In *Man, culture, and animals: the role of animals in human ecological adjustments*, edited by A. Leeds and A. P. Vayda. Washington, D.C.: American Association for the Advancement of Science.
- 1965b Camel raiding of North Arabian Bedouins: a mechanism of ecological adaptation. *American Anthropologist* 67(5): 1132–1150.
- 1969 A survey of recent Middle Eastern ethnography. *Middle East Journal* 23: 221–232.

Swett, D. H.
- 1969 Cultural bias in the American legal system. *Law and Society Review* 4: 79–110.

Sykes, G. M.
- 1969 Cases, courts and congestion. In *Law in culture and society*, edited by L. Nader. Chicago: Aldine.

Tannous, A. E.
- 1942 *The Arab village community of the Middle East.* Washington, D.C.: Annual Report of the Smithsonian Institute.

References

Task Force on Administration of Justice
  1967 *Task force report: the courts*. President's Commission on Law Enforcement and Administration of Justice. Washington, D.C.: U.S. Government Printing Office.

Todd, H. F., Jr.
  1972 *Law and conflict management in a Bavarian village*. Ph.D. dissertation, University of California, Berkeley.
  1978 Litigious marginals: character and disputing in a Bavarian village. In *The disputing process: law in ten societies*, edited by L. Nader and H. F. Todd, Jr. New York: Columbia Univ. Press.

Turner, C.
  1967 Conjugal roles and social networks: a re-examination of an hypothesis. *Human Relations* 20(2): 121–130.

Turner, V.
  1957 *Schism and continuity in an African society: a study of Ndembu village life*. Manchester: Manchester Univ. Press.

Urban Institute
  1975 *Proposal: implementation of an information and evaluation strategy for the legal services program*. Washington, D.C.

U.S. Law Enforcement Assistance Administration
  1978 *Neighborhood justice centers: an analysis of potential models*. Washington, D.C.: Office of Development, Testing and Dissemination, National Institute of Law Enforcement and Criminal Justice.

Van Velsen, J.
  1964 *The politics of kinship*. Manchester: Manchester Univ. Press.
  1967 The extended-case method and situational analysis. In *The craft of social anthropology*, edited by A. L. Epstein. London: Tavistock.

Vinogradov, A. R.
  1973 The socio-political organization of a Berber Taraf tribe: pre-protectorate Morocco. In *Arabs and Berbers: from tribe to nation in North Africa*, edited by E. Gellner and C. Micaud. London: Duckworth.
  1974 *The Ait Ndhir of Morocco: a study of the social transformation of a Berber tribe*. Ann Arbor: Univ. of Michigan, Museum of Anthropology.

Wanda, B. P.
  1975 Legal aid services in Malawi. *Washington University Law Quarterly* 1: 113–145.

Wanner, C.
  1974 The public ordering of private relations. Part I: Initiating civil cases in urban trial courts. *Law and Society Review* 8: 421–440.
  1975 The public ordering of private relations. Part II: Winning civil court cases. *Law and Society Review* 9: 293–306.

Warner, W. Lloyd et al.
  1959 *The social life of a modern community*. New Haven: Yale Univ. Press.

Waterbury, J.
  1970 *The commander of the faithful: the Moroccan political elite. A study in segmented politics*. New York: Columbia Univ. Press.

Weber, M.
  1925 *Max Weber on law in economy and society*. Cambridge, Mass.: Harvard Univ. Press. [Second edition, edited by Max Rheinstein, 1954.]

Weissman, H. H.
  1969 Problems in maintaining stability in low income social action organizations. In *Community development in the mobiliation for youth experience*, edited by H. H. Weissman. New York: Association Press.

Wiseman, J. P.
  1970 *Stations of the lost: the treatment of skid row alcoholics*. Englewood Cliffs, N.J.: Prentice-Hall.
Witty, C. J.
  1970 *Law in society: a reappraisal of perspectives*. Master's thesis, University of California, Berkeley.
  1975 *The struggle for progress: the socio-political consequences of legal pluralism*. Ph.D. dissertation, University of California, Berkeley.
  1978 Disputing issues in Shehaam, a multi-religious village in Lebanon. In *The disputing process: law in ten societies*, edited by L. Nader and H. F. Todd, Jr. New York: Columbia Univ. Press.
Wolf, E.
  1966 *Peasants*. Englewood Cliffs, N.J.: Prentice-Hall.
Yin, R. K., and D. Yates
  1975 *Street-level governments: assessing decentralization and urban services*. Lexington, Mass.: D.C. Heath.
Youssef, N. H.
  1974 *Women and work in developing societies*. Population Monograph Series No. 15. Berkeley: Univ. of California Press.
Yngvesson, B.
  1970 *Decision-making and dispute settlement in a Swedish fishing village: an ethnography of law*. Ph.D. dissertation, Univ. of California, Berkeley.
  1978 The Atlantic fishermen. In *The disputing process: law in ten societies*, edited by L. Nader and H. F. Todd, Jr. New York: Columbia Univ. Press.
Yngvesson, B., and P. Hennessey
  1975 Small claims, complex disputes: a review of the small claims literature. *Law and Society Review* 9: 219–274.
Young, M., and P. Willmott
  1957 *Family and kinship in East London*. New York: Free Press.

Index

A

Access
  to courts, 76, 79–80, 89–93, 103, 105–107, 127
  development issues, 2–3, 79–80, 132–133
  to dispute settlement, 8, 10–20, 90–91, 95–101, 102–104
  to village mediation, 59–62, 76–78, 92–93
Adjudication, 3, 6, 16, 104–105, 128, 130, 134
  alternatives to, 20, 133
  functions, 4, 18–19, 23, 123, 127
  principles and values, 3–4
  zero-sum decisions, 4, 6

B

Brokers, 6, 24–25, 91, 97–98, *see also* Political elites

C

Cases, American
  Battered Wife, 115–117
  Stolen Ring, 113–114
Cases, Lebanese
  Assault in the Fields, 87–88
  Cross-Religious Assault with a Weapon, 54–58
  Factional Insult, 40–42
  Fistfight with a Policeman, 98–99
  individual and institutional, 85
  Injured Worker, 91–92
  Insult and Violence between Women, 70–73
  Misunderstood Debt, 74–75
  Old Stone House, 37–38
  police cases, 86
  state-initiated cases, 83
  Stolen Box, 48–49
  Stolen Sheep, 49–52
  villagers', 84
Caucusing, 60, 112, 114, 116
Community
  courts, 127–130
  definitions of, 33–36, 133
  identity, 7–8, 13
  kinship, 33–36
  Middle Eastern, 11
  organization, 11, 15, 18, 23–24, 105–107, 127, 129–131
  organizing, 10–11, 131
  regional, 46–47
  self-defined levels, Shehaam, 34–35
  settlement within, 5–6, 127–134
  values, 13–16, 45–47
Conciliatory forums, 3, 11, 19, 21, 23, 76, 90
  panchayats, India, 23

153

Conciliatory forums (*cont.*)
  police, 88–89
  privacy, 11, 13, 16–17, 52, 111–112, 123, 134
Conflict management, 1, 45, 54, 130, *see also* Dispute settlement
  avoidance, 105–106, 128–130
  policy, 130–134
Courts, *see also* Adjudication
  dissatisfaction with, 8, 127
  reorganization, 127
  use of
    American, 13, 105–107, 127–129
    Lebanese, 79–80, 89–93
    the *waasta* and, 96–97, 100
Crime control model, 4
Cross-cultural comparison, 2, 4–6, 10, 23, 103, 127, 134
Cultural values
  congruent, 13–15, 46–47, 58–59
  definition of culture, 22–23
  law and, 12, 21–22, 77–78, 134
  reaffirmation, 64
  separation, 14–15, 18
  status and, 22–23

D

Development
  economic, 103
  legal, 2–3, 9, 79–80, 90–91, 93, 102–104, 131–134
  migration to cities and, 8–9
Disputants, 6, 9, 17, 60–61, 107, 110, 126
Dispute settlement
  case types, 66–67
  children's role, 49–51, 58
  compensation, 52, 55–56, 63–66
  containment value, 75–76
  crops and, 77, 82–83, 100–104
  domestic, 17–18, 60, 113–117
  participation in, 19–20, 62–63, 75–78, 92–93, 113–117
  personal aspects of, 5, 10–13, 75–76, 118, 129
  range of alternatives, 2, 100, 128–134
  as ritual, 8, 58–59
  social structure, relation to, 8–9, 78, 129, 131–134
  values in, 47–53, 75–78, 92–93, 109–110

E

Egalitarianism, 8, 16–18, 59, 77–78, 85, 125
  as ideology, 4, 10
  power differentials, 7, 16–17, 23, 73, 92–93

F

Family
  Black, 12, 14–15, 107
  court cases, 13
  courts, view of, 90–91, 129–130
  identity, 7–8, 35–36, 75–76
  Lebanese family structure, 33–39, *see also* Kinship
  nuclear family, 34
  political organization, 35–44, 92–93, 95
  urban, 10–11, 127–128, 133–134
  white working class, 12, 14–15, 107
Feuding, 77

I

Intermediation, 7, 87, 95, 101, *see also Waasta*
  women, 101–102

J

Jurisdictions
  American courts, 3–4
  conflicting, 90–91, 103
  in development, 131, 133
  Shehaam police, 29, 80, 89

K

Kinship
  and community, 33–36, 42–44, 76–77
  factions, 39–42
  marriage, 35–36
  networks, 8–9, 36–44

L

Law, 1–3, 23
  administration of, 81, 102–103, 122–123, 125, 132–134
  and development, 2–3, 9, 79–80, 90–91, 93, 102–103, 131–134
  distance from culture, 21–23, 125

Index

lawyers, 79, 91–92, 102, 134
  as protector, 4
Leadership, 8–9, 21, 23–25, 42, 47, 78, 85, 104
Legal ethnography
  development of, 1–3
  Middle Eastern, 7
  uses of, 128–134
Legal planning, 2–3, 16, 82, 92–93, 102–104, 130–134
Legitimacy, 3–4, 9, 12–13, 21–22, 46–47, 90–91, 103, 125, 130, 133

M

Mediation, *see also* Cases
  American, 8, 10–11, 23–24, 107–126
  belief in, 16, 20, 23
  case material, 68–69, 119–123
  case profile, Shehaam, 54–58
  children's use of, 74
  costs, 105–106, 122–123, 125, 128
  forms, 4–7
  functions, 7–9, 16–17, 75–78, 90–91, 93
  investigation, 62–63
  men's role, 48–53, 59–63, 73
  Middle Eastern types, 7, 48–59
  outcomes, 58–59, 68–69, 117–123, 125
  premises, 20
  principles, 10–20, 103, 109, 132
  procedures
    Shehaam, 59–62, 66, 73–75
    American, 110–117
  propositions, 20–25, 132
  referral, 107–108, 119
  rights, 90–91
  ritual, 6, 8, 58–59
  sanctions, 63–66, 125
  and social organization, 8–9, 23–25, 132–134
  therapeutic value, 5, 8, 59, 75–76, 111, 124
  theory of, 2, 10–25, 103–104, 105, 134
  time, 51, 53, 59, 75
  women's role, 61, 67–73, 115–117
Mediators, 4
  Arusha, 5
  attributes, 47, 109–113, 118
  Ifugao, 5, 7
  Kpelle, 5
  Mayors, Shehaam, 48–53, 72–73
  Ndendeuli, 5–6
  Nuer, 5

  roles of, 4–7, 55–56, 59–60, 110–113
  self-analysis, 118
  training, 109–110, 122
  Zinacantan, 9
Multiplex relations, 6, 8–10
  on-going relationships, 5–6, 10–11, 15–17, 21–24, 78, 97, 109, 122–123, 134

N

National legal system, 79–82, 90, 96–97, 100, 102–103, 112, 130, 132–134
Negotiation, 1, 6, 102, 130
Networks
  density, 33, 43
  functions, 24–25, 79, 129
  kinship, 8–9, 33, 35–40
  and mediation, 44, 59–60, 76, 92–93
  political, 35, 42–44, 95–97, 100–101
  women's, 36–39
Nurturing environment, 14

P

Police, Shehaam, 28–29, 53, 55, 62, 66, 76, 80–89
  cases, 81, 83, 84, 85, 86, 87–88
  functions, 88–89, 98–99
Political elites, 9, 21, 24–25, 76, 93, 95–100, 129, 131–132, *see also* Brokers
Political power
  factions, 39–44, 53–54, 77
  lack of, 105–106, 124, 130–131
  in mediation, 7, 70, 76–78, 92
  uses of, 35, 95–97, 133–134
  women, 39–42, 67, 101–103
Powerlessness, 17, 19, 124, 128

R

Reciprocity
  competitive resources, 24–25, 77, 85–87
  kinship, 35, 38–39, 43–44
  in mediation, 65, 134
  political, 95, 100–101

S

Sanctions, 4, 18, 63–66, 125

Scarce resources, 18–19
  competition over, 21, 24–25, 31, 85
  in Lebanese disputes, 54, 77–78, 82–83, 89
Shehaam, 27–31
  agricultural production, 28, 82–83
  community identity, 34–35
  economic relations, 100–101
  family organization, 33–44
  government relations, 35
  land, 28
  mayors, 30, 48–53, 72–73
  mediation, 54–78
  police, 28–29, 80–89
  population, 27, 29–30
  president of the municipality, 53–54
  religious life, 29–31, 34
  status markers, 45–47
Social boundaries
  ethnic, 14–15, 107, 133
  maintenance of, 39, 129, 133
  perception of, 21, 33–35, 129
  religious, 29–30, 66, 77, 84, 133
Social control, 4, 18, 47, 75–78, 82–83, 101, 125–126
  variation with law, 2, 11
Social stratification, 20, 23–25, 67, 95, 130, 134
Status, 7–8, 10, 16, 22–23, 42–43
  indicators, 45–46
Sustaining environment, 14

W

Waasta, 7, *see also* Intermediation
  functions of, 95–101
  makers, 95–98
Westernization, 2, 9, 22, 78
Witnesses, 54–55, 61–62, 80, 87, 98–99
Women
  child support, 71
  dispute case, 70–73
  and disputing, 41–42, 115–117, 125
  economic power, 35, 39
  and factions, 39
  and intermediation, 101–102
  and marriage, 35–36, 38
  and mediation, 17–18, 37–39, 40–42, 56, 61–62, 113–117
  and men, 17–18, 38–42, 60–61, 70, 102
  networks, 36–39
  political power, 39–42, 67, 101–103
  status, 45–46
  support systems, 35–36, 38–39, 41–42, 60, 72
  and work, 27–28, 31, 67, 71

Z

Zapotec, 2